Fore

When did you last put dow   , turn to
the person with you and say: "I did enjoy that. It was a
bundle of laughs!"

You don't, do you. There's so much unhappiness, so
much misery, in the newspapers these days. But if you
only knew what went into getting that news into your
newspaper, then you would see a totally different world.

In his first book, journalist and family entertainer, Peter
Brown goes behind the scenes of a typical regional
evening newspaper and reveals what really goes on. And
if that isn't enough to have you scouring the columns
of your local paper for the printing errors and the
headlines which have those dodgy double meanings
that no one has spotted until it has been too late, he
also gives a unique insight into 40 years as a semi-
professional juggler, rope-spinner and clown.

And this must go no further...

Cover photograph by courtesy of Lincolnshire Echo

Who is Peter Brown?

In the early spring of 2006, Peter took early retirement after almost 44 years as a journalist in his home city of Lincoln. His work had brought him into daily contact with the rich and the famous, the poor and the unknown and they all had a story to tell.

And in his spare evenings and days off he had a parallel career as a family entertainer, appearing all over the country first as a juggling and rope-spinning act called El Petanos and more recently as Pedro the Clown.

He also helped start an event which became one of the nation's top steam traction engine rallies, is a regular contributor to BBC Radio Lincolnshire, an after-dinner and public speaker and a long-time contributor to the showmen's weekly newspaper, World's Fair.

Peter is also very much a family man and the proud father of two daughters - born almost 31 years apart.

A few months before his retirement, he was made an Honorary Freeman of the City of Lincoln in recognition of his services.

Hold the Front Page
and Send in the Clowns

Peter Brown

Hold the Front Page and Send in the Clowns
Copyright © 2007 by Peter Brown
Library of Congress Catalogue No.

First Published in the UK by
Paul Mould Publishing
15 Standish Grove, Boston, Lincolnshire PE21 9EA
www.GetPublished.com
In association with
Empire Publishing Service
P.O. Box 1344, Studio City, CA 91614-0344
www.ppeps.com

Simultaneously published in
Australia, Canada, Germany, UK, USA

Printed in Great Britain

First Printing 2007

U.K. 9781904959-58-8
U.S.A 978158690-066-3

Chapter One

Stranger Than Fiction

The telephone rang in our office one day. It was the people from Lincoln Theatre Royal. They had booked a touring ballet company for the week and they asked if, one afternoon, we would send a photographer along to take a few pictures of the dress rehearsal.

The afternoon arrived and unfortunately - through no fault of his own - our photographer was just a little bit late getting there. But there was no problem. He knew exactly where to go and what to do. So he went round the back of the theatre, let himself in through the stage door and he walked until he reached the wings at the side of the stage. And, once he got there, he paused and he marvelled.

The rehearsal had already started. The dancers were on the stage in their costumes and tights. The lights were shining, the music was playing, the scenery was in place and they were dancing that very lovely, very moving, piece from the ballet Swan Lake.

Well, he thought, I can't possibly walk out onto the stage now and ask them to stop all this just to have their pictures taken. It wouldn't be right. So he got his camera ready and when the music was down low, he walked quietly out onto the stage.

Well, he noticed right away that one or two members of the company were looking a little bit strange at him, out of the corners of their eye - as though they hadn't quite expected him to be there.

But he thought, well obviously not everyone's

been told there's going to be a photo session this afternoon. One or two of them aren't expecting me.

So he carried on taking his pictures and he had been on the stage for a full five minutes before the horror dawned on him. There was an audience in the theatre! Five hundred children at a schools' matinee were watching him.

But he didn't panic. To his eternal credit he didn't panic. What he did was, he finished taking his pictures, did a pirouette and exited stage left. But somewhere in Lincoln, to this very day, are five hundred children still trying to work out where a Lincolnshire Echo photographer comes into the ballet Swan Lake.

Now, that perfectly true story, happened just a few years ago and I am not going to embarrass him by telling you the name of the photographer involved, because Ken James is still fondly remembered as one of the most talented photographers the Echo ever had and a perfect gentleman and it wouldn't be fair. But it does go to show that in the wonderful world of newspapers you never quite know from one minute to the next just what is going to happen.

I don't know what newspaper you take at home but when was the last time you put that newspaper down, turned to the person with you and said "By jove, I did enjoy that. That was a bundle of laughs!"

You don't, do you. There's so much misery, there's so much unhappiness in the newspapers these days. But if you only knew what went into getting that news into your newspaper, you would see a totally different world. And through the first part of this book, I would like to take you behind the scenes of the Lincolnshire Echo I used to know and tell you what really went on. And this must go no further!

But first, I started out as a junior reporter at Lincoln's weekly newspaper, called the Lincolnshire Chronicle. It was the summer of 1962. I was at the tender and impressionable age of 17 and straight from school. You couldn't do it nowadays. You would probably have to go through work experience, have a clutch of impressive A-level results to your credit and quite a bit of university experience behind you as well. But in those far off days you could join straight from school and that's what I did.

It was probably just as well that I didn't need all the A-levels because the best I could muster, after two years at the local grammar school, despite the combined efforts of some of the best teachers in Lincoln, were O-levels in English language and elementary mathematics.

Not the sort of thing to single me out for some high-flying career in the international world of business or commerce. Now the Chronicle was a very good, well-respected family newspaper with a lot of history and vast circulation area which stretched from Scunthorpe in the north to Sleaford in the south and from Gainsborough in the west to the outskirts of Skegness in the east. And we used to look after this vast section of largely rural Lincolnshire with a staff of four reporters and one photographer.

Now, being part of such a small editorial staff, was a mixed blessing because it meant that even the youngest and most inexperienced member of the staff (that was me) was thrown straight in at the deep end. So within weeks I was covering major cases at the Assizes (nowadays we call this the Crown Court), important council issues and all kinds of significant local tragedies and disasters.

To this day, I remember vividly the first words of

wisdom passed down to me by the Chronicle's sub-editor, the well-respected Geoff Fielden, as he sat behind his roll-top desk: "If you are awake you are working and if you are asleep you are dreaming about working."

Those words were to ring so very true over the years.

A lot of my training in those early days involved going out on the same jobs with more experienced reporters from the Lincolnshire Echo, which was also based in the city and later comparing the stories they wrote with my own humble version.

In those days we worked five-and-a-half days a week and two evenings, and the other three weekday evenings were filled with night school classes, where I learned good old Pitman's-style shorthand, English and, oh yes, French.

Now, just in case you may be wondering why a young reporter on a provincial weekly newspaper in the heart of Britain should need an ability to be fluent in French - in those years long before anyone ever thought about the Common Market - I should point out it was entirely due to the cost-conscious editor of the day, Mr. Franklin (who gave me my first job in journalism and for whom I will always be eternally grateful). At some stage he had made the discovery that if you sent a student to two evening classes a week at the local technical college, then you got a third evening for free.

I have got to be honest, languages have never been my strong point and I have been known to grapple unsuccessfully with even my own mother tongue on more than one occasion. And wouldn't life be dull if we all spelt exactly the same way!

Even to this day I have never succeeded in

mastering anything more than the very basics of French, and I have been grateful for the fact that just about every French person I have ever come across has had a far greater knowledge of English than I have of French.

Apart from the French classes I couldn't have done too badly I suppose, because after four years at the Chronicle, I possessed an ability to write shorthand at a speed of 100 words a minute, I had a better knowledge of English than before, and thanks to spending every Friday for a couple of years on a day release course at a Nottingham college, I had succeeded in passing my proficiency test in journalism.

It meant that I was now a qualified senior reporter and everyone expected I would immediately move on to one of those far away places with strange sounding names, like the Morning Telegraph at Sheffield, the Guardian Journal at Nottingham or the Yorkshire Post at Leeds.

Well, in the early autumn of 1966 I did move on but geographically it wasn't very far. I joined the staff of the Lincolnshire Echo, which in those days was based in St. Benedict's Square, just off the High Street. It was a red brick building, reputed to be haunted by a grey lady who, I am pretty certain, I once encountered on the top landing as I was leaving the office at eleven o'clock at night.

Every department had its own little room and the cell which made up the reporters room, had a glass roof which still bore traces of the black paint, which had been applied to meet the black-out restrictions of the Second World War.

Whenever the sun forced its way through the clouds of industrial smoke, which used to enshroud

Lincoln - before the city council, very creditably, brought in those smoke control areas - the temperature in the reporters room would rise alarmingly. To cool things down again it used to be possible to open sections of the roof by turning a big metal handle.

This worked very well until one particularly long, hot summer when somebody lost the handle and we were condemned to work in temperatures which would have put most of the tropics in the shade.

I remember one of my colleagues bringing a thermometer into the office one particularly sunny day, and complaining that by nine o'clock in the morning, it was already registering 100 degrees Fahrenheit on his desk.

Somebody, who thought he knew about these things, checked to see if the company was contravening any sort of regulation by allowing us to work under those conditions and I remember we all discovered with something of a shock, that while there appeared to be a legal minimum temperature there didn't seem to be a corresponding maximum temperature.

So there wasn't a lot we could do about it. The situation was eventually saved, to some extent, when the management installed the strangest form of ventilation system any of us had ever seen. It was an industrial, square-shaped pipe which ran the length of one wall and came to an end close to the floor, alongside the newsdesk.

The idea was that when you turned it on a powerful fan somewhere would suck the warm air out, allowing cool air to filter in.

Now, I didn't profess to know a great deal about science and physics but I always thought that warm air rises and cool air sinks, so I reckon that what the new system did was to suck out any cool air that had found its way into the room and replace it with more warm air which had been drawn down from the ceiling.

But sadly I suppose we never gave the system much of a fair trial. When you switched it on, it was so noisy that someone immediately dubbed it "the corn drier" and it was so difficult to have telephone conversation above the noise, that it was very seldom pressed into service. There didn't seem to be anything for it but to soldier on in the sweltering heat until someone found a better solution.

The solution, when it came, was something that none of us could ever have predicted. It wasn't just a proper air conditioning system. It was an entirely new office block. It was around the time when the city council was valiantly banishing traffic from large parts of the city centre and for six hours a day you couldn't legally get a vehicle to or from our offices any more. A temporary solution was found by knocking a hole through a boundary wall and creating a new access onto a passing dual carriageway.

But it was far from ideal and it became obvious that a new building was needed and fairly quickly.

It was constructed two or three stone throws away on Brayford Wharf East, alongside a much-hated railway level crossing and across the river from some run-down railway buildings and warehouses. But at least there was some limited staff parking and we all had a telephone of our own.

I remember, as a treat, we were once taken round the new building during its latter stages of construction and we had to wear hard hats as we walked up and down bare concrete staircases.

Someone official accompanied us and pointed out where internal walls would be constructed before we moved in.

When the big day arrived and it coincided with an industrial dispute which had kept us off the streets for several days, we all proudly carried our typewriters from the old office to the new one and two or three of us got into the one and only lift with a pile of office furniture - and the lift got stuck between two floors, thereby starting a tradition which was to continue on and off until the day I left.

Just before we moved into the new building, I had soared from the dizzy depths of being a senior reporter to the unthinkable. I had become the deputy news editor. Yes, I can tell you are impressed, but you have no reason to be.

I have got to say that in those days at the Lincolnshire Echo the deputy news editor was... the lowest form of animal life. When I think back to those days, I realise now that he didn't really fit in anywhere. He wasn't quite management and he wasn't quite staff. And there was only one of him.

Anyway, one of my tasks was to try to keep the news room on even keel whenever the news editor took a day off or had a holiday. Well, I suppose, we did keep on even keel but occasionally we sailed through some very choppy waters. And one particular time happened on a Saturday in early September.

Now nobody, nobody at all, likes working on a Saturday and Lincolnshire Echo reporters and photographers were no exception. But because the paper came out six days a week, we had to have a staff on duty right through the weekend and this time it was my turn to be in charge.

A job came onto the office diary that had to be covered. There was a charity raft race starting off at Torksey Lock on the River Trent at lunchtime and throughout the afternoon these home-made rafts were paddling their way down the Fossdyke canal and they were due to arrive in Brayford Pool, right in the very middle of Lincoln, at about five o'clock in the afternoon.

Obviously we needed to be there to see who won the race. So I asked one of our young reporters, a lad called Paul, if he would go along and cover the arrival of these rafts. Normally Paul was very keen, very willing and very eager. But this time he didn't want to go. It was a lovely sunny day and I think he wanted to get off early and spend the rest of the weekend with his family, which was fair enough. And all day he moaned, he cringed and he whinged and once or twice I was very tempted to say: "Don't go, Paul. Ring somebody up on Monday morning and find out what happened."

But I didn't. I stuck to my guns and I am glad I did because what happened was something nobody could have expected.

At four o'clock, Paul left the office, very miserable, very down at heel. He still didn't want to go.

He came back half-an-hour later, and I had never seen him so excited in his life. He had run all the way from Brayford Pool (admittedly not very far but there were two flight of stairs involved at the end) and what had happened was something nobody could have expected.

Those were the days when Brayford Pool was surrounded by those floating wooden pontoons all around the edge. These floating wooden pontoons were soundly constructed. They were a monument

9

to British craftsmanship.

But they weren't constructed to carry the weight of people. And as the rafts entered Brayford Pool at the far end, all the dignitaries and VIPs decided to go down onto these floating wooden pontoons to get a better look and as more and more of them went onto the floating wooden pontoons they sank lower and lower into the water.

Nobody saw who won the race. Nobody was bothered. They were all too intent on watching the VIPs coming out of the water, soaked to the skin.

The manager of Lincoln City Football Club at the time, was one of them, and that somehow seemed to make things even better.

But the beauty of that story was that nobody got hurt. One or two people had their pride dented but even they had a good laugh about it later on and that's just the sort of story we all loved to write about and to read.

And I remember something very similar to that happened in the mid to late 1960s.

Depending on where you live, you may or may not have heard about Lincoln Music Festival. It has been running for thousands and thousands of years in Lincoln (and I am a journalist, I do not exaggerate!)

And you might have thought that after all these years, nothing unexpected or untoward could ever happen in the well-ordered world of Lincoln Music Festival.

Well, you would be wrong. You would be very wrong.

It was taking place in the Central Methodist Church in Lincoln High Street. It's a big church and it was packed. The massed choirs had gathered from all over the diocese to sing as one.

The conductor, who was very well known in music circles - he had come all the way from London - rose to his feet, climbed the stairs to the rostrum. All eyes were on him. You could have heard a pin drop.

He picked up his baton, thrust his arms in the air with all the strength he could muster. His braces went and his trousers came down.

And the choir carried on singing.

Newspapers throughout the country carried that story. And one newspaper as far away as Australia, even had a cartoon about it.

So it does go to show that in the wonderful world of the newspapers, you never really do know from one minute to the next just what is going to happen.

Chapter Two

My Close Encounter with a Lion

There isn't another career in the world quite like being a newspaper reporter. It gives you instant job satisfaction. Something you write in the morning can be in the newspaper and read before the end of the day and I never quite got over that thrill.

Many a time I would lurk in the High Street and watch someone buy a copy of the Echo from a newspaper stand and casually thumb through the pages. Whenever he reached one of my stories, I had the greatest temptation to rush over to him and scream: "I wrote that!"

I never did actually do that to a member of the public, of course, but I have got to admit I was very, very tempted.

After a couple of decades at the Echo, the editor of the day - who, I have got to be say, never really liked me - decided I ought to have a career change, so he moved me off newsdesk to a new post which he had created and laughingly dubbed Leisure and Entertainments Editor. To this day I am still not entirely sure what it meant but just to soften the blow he added £5 a week to my salary for doing it.

To be honest, whatever his motives were, he couldn't have done me a greater favour. I had never seen myself as a born leader of men (or women, for that matter). I always had the greatest difficulty in getting people to do what I wanted and more often than not it was so much easier to simply do the job myself than to spend a long time trying to tell someone else how to do it.

And sometimes, when you looked around the quality and the quantity of reporters we had available at any one time to cover the stories which came in, it was often difficult to match one up with another. I don't mean for one moment that they weren't up to the job. Far from it. Many of them were far too good for the jobs I was having to ask them to cover. Sometimes you almost felt it was a bit like asking a thoroughbred racehorse to take part in a donkey derby. The young John Inverdale, for instance, who had his first job at the Echo before going off to BBC Radio Lincolnshire and later on to national television, was excellent when it came to covering sport and most kinds of features. But it somehow never seemed quite right wasting him on a garden fete or a magistrates court that you knew was going to be full of stories about motorists who had driven the wrong way down a one way street or of cyclists who had dared to risk life and limb by pedalling through the city streets without lights after dark.

There was one young reporter we had, who came to us straight from university and I don't doubt that in his particular field of expertise he was a real whiz. Unfortunately, even after several years, I never really did discover what that field of expertise was. His time-keeping left a bit to be desired as well and when he eventually tumbled in through the newsroom door one morning in the run-up to Christmas, I remarked that he reminded me of that line from that much-loved carol, Hark the Herald Angels Sing.

"Oh yes," he said, looking almost interested for once. "What line is that?"

"Late in time behold him come," I replied.

The twenty-one years I was to spend as Leisure and Entertainments Editor were the happiest times of my life in journalism. I no longer had to deal with the nasty side of life. I could turn a blind eye to all the disasters, the tragedies, the boring council meetings that went on into the night and the complicated court hearings that interfered with my dinner hour, knowing that some other unfortunate person was going to have to write about them and I could at last concentrate on the happier side of life.

Part of my time was spent sorting through the television and radio programme schedules, picking out some of the more interesting and writing little features about them. Now, I have never considered myself being particularly good at watching television. I have a very low boredom thresh-hold, especially when it comes to the soaps. It was at that point I realised just how dreadful some of the programmes could be and on more than one occasion I would crumple the sheets of programme schedules up into a ball, and toss it into the bin with the anguished words: "I can't write about any television highlights tonight, because there aren't any!"

I suppose that if you spend a large part of your working day, dealing with the television schedules and wading through innumerable press releases about the forthcoming programmes, then you don't spend a large part of your spare time watching them. It's probably the same principle that if you work in a crisp factory you don't eat crisps and if you are employed at a chocolate factory, then you don't eat chocolate.

The rest of my time during this period was spent, far more productively, writing a diary column called The Gossiper.

If I could have had my way, I would rather it had been called something else but the title had first been created, I think, way back in the 1920s and it had survived through at least one world war, a recession or two and countless other disasters. So The Gossiper it remained. And, I suppose, there was a strange sort of poetic justice to the fact that I became The Gossiper as well, because of something that happened during those mercifully short few weeks between my leaving school and starting work.

For a fortnight during the summer, I was part of a team of youngsters employed by the council to conduct a traffic census through the city streets. The first week was spent dutifully counting the number of vehicles to pass a given point on their way into the city centre. The second was just a little more challenging. You congregated at the short stretch of dual carriageway at arguably Lincoln's busiest road junction.

Every time the traffic lights at the junction turned to red you knew you had perhaps the best part of two minutes before they changed to green again and the traffic carried on along its way. During that time, armed with the inevitable clip board, a list of questions and a pen, you had to approach the driver of the nearest car and ask him all manner of intelligent questions, like where his journey had started, where he was heading for, did he always use that route and whether the journey was for business or pleasure.

Most drivers were helpful, which was a great benefit to me because as a spotty faced, seventeen-year-old straight out of grammar school, I still possessed more than a hint of shyness. But I well remember one man I approached. He was at the wheel of an expensive-looking car and he must have regarded it as something of an affront to be approached by a boy with an unfashionable crew-cut, because hardly had I had a chance to explain what it was all about, than he demanded to know how much money I was getting paid for asking these, what he considered to be, pointless questions.

In all innocence I told him immediately. Looking back, I think I must have been rather proud of the amount but I remember he looked horrified.

"That's far too much. It's a waste of public money," he interrupted, in no uncertain terms. "I'm going to write to The Gossiper about this."

And he wound his window up and drove off in a right old state.

I never forgot the incident and something like two decades later, when I took over the mantle of Gossiper, it gave me enormous pleasure to think that if the same thing had happened all those years later, he would have been writing to me.

Being the author of The Gossiper page had other good points as well.

At last I was able to concentrate on the nicer side of life. There was a lot of nostalgia. There was the chance for me to express an opinion or two. We reunited friends and relatives who hadn't seen one another for a long time and on one memorable occasion it seems I was even instrumental in bringing together a lovely couple who hadn't seen one another for decades. Although by now they were both widowed and well beyond their first flush of youth, they soon realised they still had strong feelings for one another and I was thrilled when they invited me to their wedding at a pretty little country church not far from Lincoln, a few months afterwards.

But just occasionally The Gossiper page - which I

always regarded as a little oasis of nice stories among a desert of nasty news - did get me into some strange places.

For instance have you ever said something on the spur of the moment and regretted it straight away?

We have all done it at one time or another, haven't we. This happened to me in the late 1980s. Gerry Cottle's Circus was coming to Lincoln South Common and the week before the show came to town the advance manager came into the Echo office and we had a meeting about the kind of stories we might do while the circus was here.

And there was a lull in the conversation and for some reason, to this day I am still not quite sure why I did it, I found myself asking the man from the circus: "I don't suppose there's any chance of me going into the lions' cage when you are in Lincoln?"

Straight away I could have bitten my tongue out. But the man from the circus looked at me in a very strange way and said: "Oh, I don't know, Peter, we have never done that."

Then I think he thought he had better humour me. So he said: "If you like - if you really like - and I think you are mad but if you really like, when I get back to the circus tonight, I'll ask Martin Lacey. They are his lions. I will see what he says, and I will give you a ring tomorrow."

Well, I thought, I am all right. I remember Martin Lacey. Used to watch him on television when I was younger. Zoo Time, Don't Ask Me, Magpie, all the other programmes. I thought there is no way a man like him will have me in his lions' cage. I am quite all right. Until the phone went the next day and it was the man from the circus.

"No problem. You can come into the lions' cage

any morning that we are in Lincoln."

His words echoed round my head like machine gun bullets. I noticed that, although I was sitting down, my knees were starting to knock. But I wasn't in the cage yet and I didn't really believe I ever would be. I had been thinking about this overnight (like you would) and I had thought up a get-out so I wouldn't have to go and I wouldn't have to lose face. So, quick as a flash, I said: "That is wonderful news. Thank you very much indeed. And obviously, yes, I really do want to go into the lions' cage (No doubt about that). But I had just better go and have a word with the Editor because he may not want me to do it."

So I went in to see the Editor - in his den - on all fours, like you did. And he looked down on me from on high and I looked up at him and explained in a tiny, tiny voice what had happened. And for one moment, just for one moment, I thought he hadn't heard me. Then he threw himself back in his chair. I had never heard him laugh so much in all his life. In the end, he wiped the tears from his eyes and said: "What a wonderful idea. Of course you can do it!"

By now the noose was beginning to tighten around my neck. But I wasn't there yet. The Editor had a little think and he said: "You had better go up to the accounts department to make sure you are going to be covered by the insurance."

Now, wouldn't you have thought that in the Echo's public liability insurance policy there would have been some tiny, tiny words in tiny, tiny print somewhere that say: "Thou shalt not cause a member of the editorial staff to enter a cage of lions."

Well, there wasn't. They never thought it would happen so they never wrote it into the insurance policy.

So the next week the circus has arrived on the South Common. The tent is there. In the middle of the tent is the ring. In the middle of the ring is the lions' cage. In the middle of the lions' cage is my desk, that somebody has kindly brought down from the office. My chair is there. My typewriter is there. My telephone is there. Even the litter bin is there. And the idea is I am going to write the day's Gossiper stories from inside this lions' cage.

Now, I am no fool, although there's no need to take a vote on it. So I thought, before I go into the lions' cage I had better get some words of wisdom from the great man himself, Martin Lacey. And Martin looked at me, in the way that he does, and he said: "Now Peter, I don't want my lions to feel threatened!"

I thought: "You have got to be joking. There is no way I am ever going to threaten a fully-grown male African lion."

But he said: "This is their home and this is their territory. Now they don't know you and they may well feel threatened. There are two danger signals to look out for. One is if the lion yawns. And the other one is if the lion turns away from you."

This is perfectly true and it works exactly the same at home with your own pet ginger Tom. If he is out in the back garden and a dog walks by or another cat comes into the garden, he may well feel threatened and the chances are he will yawn and he will turn away. Well, it's just the same with lions - only on a rather bigger scale.

I am sitting at my desk in the lions' cage. The Echo photographer has not joined us. On this occasion he has decided to take his pictures from the outside, looking in. Five feet away from my right shoulder is this lion. And he is a lovely lion. If you were to sit down now and draw a picture of your ideal lion, that is the one you would draw. They used him on television adverts for Peugeot cars. He was on Lion King chocolate bars. He advertised Superking Cigarettes. He was in that film, American Werewolf in London. He is a famous lion but he is still a lion, and he is still five feet away from my right shoulder.

I looked over my shoulder and he is yawning. Now, what did Martin say about yawning lions? I thought, well maybe he's feeling a bit tired. Perhaps he went out last night and didn't get back until the early hours. Then I thought, no lions don't go out, do they. Or if they do then we tend to hear about it the next day.

So I carried on working, and I happened to glance over my shoulder again, and the lion is turning away from me.

Now, I thought, what did Martin say about lions turning away from me? But no, I was quite safe, and under Martin's expert guidance I finished writing my Gossiper story, left the cage completely unharmed and I went home, feeling pretty pleased with myself.

That night, for no reason at all, my dear little pet tabby cat - who I loved very much - suddenly gets off the settee, pads quietly across the floor towards me and gives me quite a vicious scratch all the way down the back of my hand. There's blood. Quite a lot of blood.

So the next morning, having survived my ordeal in the lions' cage, I go into the Echo office, my hand covered in bandages, having been savaged by my own pet tabby cat.

Life can be so very, very cruel.

The lions' cage wasn't the only unusual spot I found myself in during those years at the Echo. For instance, can you envisage a situation where you would end up in bed with a female colleague, being photographed by a cameraman and it would all be perfectly innocent?

It happened in the bedding department of the local Co-op department store. Our health reporter was doing a piece about husbands or wives who snored and the effect it could have on their partners. The story was fine but she needed a picture to accompany her words of wisdom and it wasn't the sort of thing you could invite a member of the public to do. So - I can't quite member how it happened, whether I volunteered for it or not - it was arranged that one of my colleagues and I would pose for the picture in a local store.

With the co-operation of the bemused bedding department staff, I remember I peeled off my shirt, tie and shoes and hopped into one of the double beds on display. I was joined, a few moments later by my colleague, who had taken the time and trouble to put her hair in rollers and to put on a nightie top. We then spent an hilarious ten minutes or so, as the photographer did his best to keep a straight face and took pictures of me pretending to be asleep while my colleague sat up in bed glaring at me.

Now, I am a great giggler, and at times of crisis and tension, I go off into uncontrollable fits of laughter, and this was one of those occasions. Tears were pouring down my face by the time we finished but the pictures came out all right and that was the main thing.

And that wasn't the only time I posed for a picture for a health story. Sometime after the snoring feature, our reporter penned a tale about the dangers of accidents around the home, and she dreamed up this scenario of some unfortunate person laying in the bath with their toe stuck in the tap.

Come on, that sort of thing must happen all the time. Once again I was assigned to pose for the picture, so armed with a pair of swimming trunks and a towel and a yellow plastic duck, to make the whole thing look even more realistic, I set off for the nearest bathroom fittings showroom on one of the city's trading estates.

Unfortunately the only suitable baths they had were on display in the shop window. It was tea time and there were a lot of people walking by on their way home from work but having made the trip along with one of our photographers, there could be no question of backing out or postponing it until the middle of the night when there was no one else around.

So I stripped off in the staffroom, left my clothes there and padded through the crowded showroom to the window, wearing only a pair of swimming trunks, a towel draped casually around my shoulders and clutching a yellow plastic duck in my hand.

Now, wouldn't you have thought that in a showroom, crowded with shoppers, this might have caused just a little bit of a stir? Well, it didn't. Not a bit of it. Nobody turned their heads. Nobody even batted an eyelid, as far as I could see. I walked all the way through the showroom, spent the next few minutes in the bath in the window, got out and walked all the way back to the staffroom again and there was no reaction from anybody. Aren't the British public magnificent.

Chapter Three

You Had to Laugh!

One of my little chores at the Echo was to try to make sure we didn't upset too many of our readers, because unlike the national newspapers (with the greatest respect to them) our readers were very close to us geographically and we knew that if we got something even remotely wrong, the person we had offended would, quite properly, have been down in our reception the next day - or the same day sometimes - hammering on the desk saying: "You have got this wrong. Please put it right." Or words to that effect. And if it was our fault we would put our hands on our hearts and say: "Very sorry we won't do it again," and we would put in a correction as soon as possible.

But occasionally, when things went wrong, it wasn't through the fault of any member of the staff, because when people are talking to a newspaper reporter they occasionally say things that can be taken in two different ways and it is not until they see the story in print that they realise what they have done.

I shall never forget the time when there was a caravan fire on the Lincolnshire holiday coast. Nothing too serious but a small touring caravan had been damaged by fire and another caravan parked close by had been damaged by smoke. Nobody had been hurt. But an eyewitness was describing to one of our reporters just what had happened. He said, and I quote; "It was terrible. It was just like in that film... The Towering Inferno."

I remember The Towering Inferno - just. I thought: "I am going over to Skegness because I have never ever seen a 600-storey caravan... especially not a touring one."

But it does go to show that people can and do say things they don't exactly mean. Like the time I was interviewing this lovely lady, in a village not far from Lincoln. She had started a club to serve the people of her community and she was telling me the marvellous, marvellous facilities they had on offer.

She said: "We have bingo, we have darts, we have pool and we have snooker." And she went on (and I quote): "The snooker table is very popular. There's always a big queue (cue)!"

Quite honestly, you couldn't invent a pun like that, could you. It's got to be spontaneous.

There was a time in my career when I was the editorial training officer, which sounds an impressive job and I suppose it was important in its way but there was no extra money involved. It was the sort of job they thrust upon you because they suspected you might have more time to spare than anybody else.

One lesson I would always try to get over to anyone when they just joined us was: "If anything can be misunderstood, there is someone, somewhere who will misunderstand it."

And I would illustrate it with this story which happened in Lincoln some years ago. The headmaster of one of the junior schools, not far from the cathedral, hit on this marvellous idea of sending his senior boys and girls out into the community, armed with a notebook and pen, to interview some aged relative about the war. Then the idea was the pupils would go back to school and write an essay for the school magazine, just like a real newspaper reporter.

Well, this little lad went off to see his Grandad, and he said: "Grandad, Grandad, you fought in the war, didn't you."

And his Grandad replied: "Yes, that's right son, I was there."

The lad took out his notebook and said: "Grandad can I ask you a few questions for a story for the school magazine? When it was all over, did you bring any souvenirs home with you?"

Grandad thought for a moment and he said: "Yes, of course I did. We all did."

"Well, what did you bring?" demanded the boy. "Did you bring any ammunition?"

Grandad looked a bit guilty and then he said: "Well yes I did, actually. I don't want this generally known but there's some bullets I got from a German soldier we captured. Let me think. They will be upstairs in one of the drawers."

And the little lad wrote it down in his notebook. Then he said: "Grandad, Grandad, did you bring any weapons home with you?"

"Well, yes I did," he confessed. "There's my old army service revolver. That's upstairs in one of the cupboards."

Again, the little lad wrote it down. Then he said: "Grandad, Grandad, did you bring any uniform home with you?"

"Yes I did," he replied. "There's my old army tunic. That's upstairs in the attic.. on the tank."

The little boy looked astounded. "You brought a tank home with you?"

It just goes to show that if something can be misunderstood, there will be someone, somewhere who will misunderstand it.

Now place names have always fascinated me, and

in Lincolnshire we have got some beauties. There's Mavis Enderby, Tanvats, Thompson's Bottom, Pode Hole to name but a few and, oh yes, there's even a Spittal-in-the-Street, which I always think sounds a bit like an offence.

But if we have got them in Lincolnshire, then they have got them in other parts of the country as well, and they all pose a problem for the local journalist. For instance, did you know (and I bet you did) that in Kent, there is a village called Loose. There's nothing funny about that, until you realise that they have got in this village of Loose, a Women's Institute. I often wondered how they reacted to being called "Loose women".

Just outside Bradford is a suburb called Idle. Again nothing funny about that until you happen to discover that they have got in Idle, a Working Men's Club, and I suspect they must do very well selling membership forms to people who want to belong to "The Idle Working Men's Club."

If I ever became a medical practitioner, I always thought I would probably set up my surgery in the village of Healing, not far from Grimsby, because then I would forever be known as "A Healing doctor."

In a county some miles south of Lincolnshire, there are neighbouring villages. One village is called Yelling, and then a few miles down the road you have got the hamlet of Ugeley. Now again, there's nothing funny about that, until the day a man from one village married a lady from the next village, and the local paper came up with the headline: "Yelling man marries Ugeley woman."

The Echo and the Chronicle, like just about every other local newspaper in the country, relied to a large extent on a team of poorly-paid village correspondents to keep them informed about what was going on at a local level. And by and large they were wonderful, wonderful people, because they knew everybody in their village, everybody knew them, their finger was on the pulse of the community and they were great and marvellous ambassadors for us.

But, just like you and me, they occasionally said and wrote things that could be taken two different ways. Like the time one of our correspondents submitted a report of her annual village produce show, which contained the golden line: "Mrs. Bradshaw entered the winning pork pie."

Now, if you think about that for a moment, we are talking quite literally, a very tiny Mrs. Bradshaw or very large pork pies with doors in them.

And at around the same time, one of my colleagues wrote a story which contained the sentence: "All the dead fish in the River Witham are going to be replaced by farmers."

Don't you just get a wonderful mental picture of those farmers in their green wellies, floating down the river?

But that's nothing compared to a story which appeared in a Lincoln parish magazine once, which contained the sentence: "During the Easter Sunday service, the Vicar's wife will lay an egg on the altar!"

I wanted to be there. You could have sold tickets.

National newspapers aren't above this sort of thing either, thank goodness. How often do we read: "A man was found guilty of murder at Crown Court." That can't be right, or if it is, why didn't any of the police, barristers or even the judge try to stop him from committing the crime? Surely that should read: "At Crown Court, a man was found guilty of murder."

If we think back, we have all read headlines like: "Miners refuse to work after death", "War dims hopes of peace" and "Prostitutes appeal to Pope".

And what about my own personal favourite: "Stolen painting found by tree."

Well, clever tree! Police all over the county have been looking for this stolen artwork, and it took a tree to find it.

Even our dear friends at BBC Radio Lincolnshire have been known to do something similar from time to time and I think I can tell this story against them because they are ever so kind to me and quite regularly I am invited along to one of the programmes and we have a bit of fun recalling some events from the past.

One day I heard one of their newsreaders, say in all seriousness: "Elderly people in Lincolnshire are being urged to have flu jabs, by Henry Cooper."

Now I admire Henry Cooper. I really do. But if I ever have a flu jab it will be done by a qualified doctor and not by a former boxing champion.

I always found that one of the nicest parts about working in newspapers was having the chance to meet celebrities from the field of showbusiness, politics and sport. And not just meeting them but having interviews with them either face to face or on the end of a telephone. Over the years I was so very, very lucky to have met and interviewed some marvellous, marvellous people.

But one that I shall never forget, was something of a first for British journalism, the day that I did a telephone interview with... Sooty!

All right, you are going to say that Sooty doesn't talk so how could he have done a telephone interview with him. Well, we cheated just a little bit. Sooty was coming to the Theatre Royal in Lincoln, with a lovely lady called Connie Crighton. Now, whenever you didn't see the late Harry Corbett or Matthew, Connie was the lady who, quite often, was hand in glove with Sooty. And she's as daft as I am. She really is.

The week before she came to Lincoln, she was appearing at a theatre in Derby and it was arranged that I would do this telephone interview with her from our office. Now, I have got to explain, I worked in a vast open-plan office. It was a bit like Tesco's - only without the special offers. At almost any hour of the day or night there could have been as many as forty people working on this floor. Normally it was a very busy, very noisy place, until the precise moment you were about to start an embarrassing or dodgy telephone conversation and then a deafly hush would descend upon the entire floor and forty pairs of ears would hone in on what you were saying.

It was uncanny and that's what happened to me this day. But I was not going to be put off. So, summoning up as much dignity as I could, I said: "Connie, can you tell me, is Sooty as naughty off-stage as he is on?"

And, Connie, in all seriousness, is replying: "Oh yes, Peter, he's just as naughty off-stage as he is on."

And I find myself saying: "Can Sooty hear what we are saying about him, Connie?"

This is a grown man talking to a grown woman!

At around the same time, I was very lucky to have the chance to interview a character called Postman Pat. Do you know, I had never heard of Postman Pat, but if you tell a child you have talked to him, you go up in their estimation. You become a demi-God. "Well, Postman Pat was coming to the Ritz Theatre in Lincoln High Street. Years later it became a bar, and what a tragedy for Lincoln that they ever lost that place for live entertainment. It was magnificent.

The week before Postman Pat came to the city, it was arranged I would do this telephone interview with him from the office and at the precise moment when I am about to dial the number, the deafly hush has descended again and everyone is listening in.

But I am not going to be put off. Oh no I am not. By now I have had the opportunity to do some research into this Postman Pat. I have got some pertinent questions to ask of him and I want some answers.

So I said: "Postman Pat, who's going to be delivering the mail in your village, when you are going to be here in Lincoln all next week?" And: "How's your black and white cat?"

A lifetime in newspapers, and I wanted to know how his cat was!

Sometimes you found yourself talking to sporting celebrities and many years ago now - just before his very sad death - I was very lucky to have the chance to interview a legend of the wrestling world; a giant of a man called Big Daddy. Now with Big Daddy, as nice as he was and he really was a perfect gentleman, you had a little bit of a problem, and the problem came with the name. Think about it. Once you had introduced yourself and you had said: "Hello Big Daddy," how could you shorten it the next time? I couldn't work it out. You couldn't just call him "Big." You couldn't call him "Daddy" or even "Dad."

Yes, his real name was Shirley Crabtree but there was no way I was ever going to call a giant wrestler "Shirley". I called him Big Daddy the whole way through the conversation and he didn't seem to mind at all. What a wonderful character he was and I don't

30

think the sport of wrestling ever quite got over his passing.

But sometimes the celebrities would turn the tables on you and ask you a question that you weren't expecting and you couldn't answer. Like the day I was doing an interview with an actor called David McCallum. Do you remember David McCallum? He was in Sapphire and Steel, The Man From U.N.C.L.E, The Invisible Man, Colditz, The Great Escape, The Mosquito Squadron and all the rest of them.

He was coming to the Theatre Royal in a Shakespeare production and the week before he arrived, we did this telephone interview from the office. Now, looking back, I think he must have allocated more time for the interview than I had.

Because I had asked him all my questions. He had given me some lovely answers. We had had a wonderful conversation and I was all set to say: "Thank you very much, David, it's been a real pleasure."

But before I could, he said: "Peter, just before you go, there's something I would like to ask you. A little bit of local knowledge. I have never been to Lincoln before and if I get any spare time next week, I would love to go somewhere for a game of golf. But I don't know the area at all. So where would you recommend?"

Now, I have got to tell you, he was talking to the wrong man. Only once in my life have I ever set foot on a golf course and been allowed to live. But I wasn't going to admit this to the famous David McCallum. So I am desperately, desperately trying to think of all the golf courses I have ever driven past, read about or heard people talking about and I started to reel them off as if I really knew what I was saying. You would have been so proud.

I said: "There's a championship golf course at Woodhall Spa - a lot of people go there. There's one recently opened at Martin Moor. Lincoln's got some nice ones - there's Southcliffe and Carholme - and, oh yes, you mustn't forget Torksey, that's very nice."

So he said: "Yes, I like the sound of Torksey. Do you think if I mention your name I will get a game?"

Yes he did, and I was so tempted. Can you imagine, this international film star turning up at the gates of Torksey Golf Club, winding down the window of his Rolls Royce and telling the man in charge: "Oh, it's all right. I know Peter Brown from the Lincolnshire Echo."

I was so tempted but I didn't. I said: "I am sure you will get a game without mentioning my name, David," and I have no doubt that he did.

Sometimes, an interview with a celebrity would take place at a crowded press conference, where you would hope to shout one or two questions that might just be picked up above the general barrage of words being voiced by colleagues from other sections of the media. But I remember going to one press conference at a Nottingham ice rink, some years ago, when there were probably a dozen other young reporters there, and nobody seemed prepared to ask the first question.

The celebrities were Britain's top ice dancing champions, Jane Torville and Christopher Dean, who were about to return to their home city with a spectacular show before going off on a national tour.

And after what was fast becoming a very embarrassing silence for everybody in the room, I eventually piped up with the first question which was prefaced with the words: "Can I just break the ice by asking..."

After that, the questions came thick and fast, and I suspect my fellow journalists had decided not to give me the opportunity to make another dreadful joke.

Looking back, I think one of the most difficult face to face interviews I have ever done with any celebrity was some years ago now, with a gentleman called Harvey Smith. Why is it that whenever you mention his name in public a little smile runs round the faces of your audience?

Poor Harvey Smith. For years he has been one of the nation's top showjumping champions. Honours and trophies galore must litter the walls of his home. But what is he remembered for above all else? Yes, it's that defiant two-fingered gesture he did at Hickstead all those years ago. Now what made him so very difficult to interview - and I don't want to upset or offend anyone by saying this - but what made Harvey so very difficult to interview is that he is a Yorkshiremen. And if Yorkshire people had any faults (which they haven't) but if Yorkshire people had any faults it would be that they are economical with words.

And Harvey was very economical with words.

He was doing a Sunday evening appearance at the Embassy Centre on the seafront at Skegness one very cold Sunday evening in January and it was arranged that one of our photographers and I would go over to the theatre and interview him on the stage before the audience came in. I had thought up about twenty questions to ask him and I considered that I would be very lucky to get through half-a-dozen of them, because I was convinced that once I had started him talking, I would never be able to shut him up.

So I asked him the first question. I said: "Harvey,

does the adrenalin flow in the same way before you go onto the stage, as it does before you go into the competition ring?"

And I thought that's a fair question for starters.

Harvey looked up into the air. He looked down at his feet. He looked back up into the air again. He stroked his chin. He thought for a moment and he said: "Yes" - in a very strong Yorkshire accent. Just the one word.

Well, I thought, I have started now so things shouldn't be quite so difficult. So I asked him the next question. I said: "Which is easier Harvey? Is it easier going onto a stage and entertaining an audience, like you will be doing this evening or is it easier riding one of your magnificent horses for Britain?"

Harvey looked up into the air. He looked down at his feet. He looked back up into the air again. He stroked his chin. He thought for a moment and he said: "This is."

And that was it. We went right through the entire conversation, all twenty questions, and only a one or two word reply to every one of them. In the end, he had his pictures taken, we left the stage and the audience came into the theatre. We stayed to listen to his talk and he was very entertaining.

Although you don't see him on the television quite so much these days and you don't hear him so often on the radio, whenever I do, I still have the greatest sympathy for the poor reporter who is asking those questions.

Sometimes, when you are doing an interview with a celebrity, it crosses your mind that he or she may not be telling you the truth, but because it's virtually impossible to prove at the time and because it sounds such a good story, you don't really go to a lot of trouble to challenge it. So, I confess, you do tend to take a lot of things at their face value.

One very hot and sunny Spring Bank Holiday Monday (yes, they do happen from time to time), in the mid-1960s, the Chronicle staged Lincoln's first open-air pop festival at the City Football Ground. It was very much a ground-breaking event and one of the forerunners of the many and larger open-air pop festivals that we all know and love to this day. Looking down the list of stars who were appearing during a 10-hour session, it seemed as if everyone who was anyone, was there.

There were The Who, The Kinks, The Yardbirds, The Barron Knights, The Ivy League, Screaming Lord Sutch (long before he had aspirations of a political career) and Georgie Fame to name but a few. And one of the comperes was the rapidly-rising star, Jimmy Saville.

I remember he was just a little bit late getting to the Sincil Bank Stadium and when I interviewed him before he went on stage, he told me this far-fetched tale about how he was staying at what was Lincoln's top hotel and how on his way to the festival he had got stuck in the lift. The story was accompanied by all those lavish gestures and cigar-waving movements that became his trademark and at the end of it all I was left wondering: "Did that really happen or was he just spinning me a yarn for the sake of a good story?"

It was to be 32 years before I would discover the answer.

During the summer of 1998, I was on holiday in Scarborough with a young lady, called Lynn, who was later to become my wife. We were enjoying an evening meal in a restaurant, when a gentleman with long blond hair came in and began strolling round, talking to customers in general. He looked vaguely familiar and when he approached our table, we recognised him immediately as Jimmy Saville.

He seemed in no rush to move away, so I reminded him of our previous meeting when he was in Lincoln for the pop festival and he immediately recalled: "Oh yes, that's when I got stuck in the hotel lift!"

My faith in the honesty of the rich and the famous was immediately restored.

But sometimes stories are eventually proved to be a hoax or even a pack of lies, and the most elaborate hoax that I ever fell victim of (to my knowledge at least) happened during my time as Gossiper at the Lincolnshire Echo. It was quite simply the story that never was - although it was more than a year before I discovered the truth.

It started the day I received a phone call at the office. As occasionally happened, the man declined to give his name, for what he called personal reasons. But he sounded a mature sort of character and during the conversation he let slip the fact that he lived in Branston, a village not far from Lincoln.

The story he began to tell me was so unlikely that it just had to be true, because I couldn't at the time see how or why anyone would want to make it up. During the course of what was a very long phone call, he told me he had been a choir boy at Lincoln Cathedral during the Second World War and one night, when his father and mother were attending a service and the Bishop himself was preaching, a heavily-laden Lancaster bomber took off from Skellingthorpe airfield, on the edge of Lincoln.

The aircraft was on its way to enemy-occupied

Europe and as he struggled to gain height, the pilot could see the triple towers of Lincoln Cathedral getting ever closer on the hilltop in front of him. When he realised he wasn't going to clear the towers, he did the only possible thing he could and he flew his Lancaster between the central tower and the two smaller towers.

My informant assured me it was such a near thing that as the aircraft skimmed the top of the cathedral roof, one of its wheels caught the top of it, broke off and crashed to the ground.

The Lancaster was supposed to have continued on its way to the continent but never returned from its mission.

By any standards, it was an amazing story and the only thing that troubled me just a little bit was why I had never heard about it before. After all there must have been a lot of people in the cathedral for the service and surely the tale would have become a part of the city's history.

But the caller told me they hadn't made a lot of it at the time because of security and the crew of the Lancaster hadn't lived to tell the tale.

After thinking about it for a few days, I ran the story on The Gossiper page and hoped that a reader, who might have been in the cathedral at the time, would get in touch to verify the tale. Sure enough, it wasn't long before I started getting letters from people living in places like Nottingham and Doncaster, who backed up the story and I ran subsequent reports based on the letters.

One woman, claiming to have been a member of the W.A.A.F. during the war, wrote to say she remembered going to the cathedral to collect the damaged wheel. It all seemed to be adding up.

But I still had a niggling doubt. Every time I went by the cathedral, I found myself looking up at the space between the towers and trying to work out if there really was room to get a Lancaster bomber between them in the dark.

I even wrote a piece, tongue-in-cheek, to suggest that next time the nation's only flying Lancaster bomber, which now forms part of the Coningsby-based Battle of Britain Memorial Flight, was in the air, the pilot might just give it a bit of a go to see if it was possible.

My friend, former Fleet Street journalist, the late Trevor Reynolds, who had semi-retired to Lincolnshire, read the story and decided to put it to the test. He sat down in front of his computer, fed quite a bit of information into it, and decided that yes it would have been just about possible to have flown a Lancaster bomber between the towers - but only just.

Again the story had taken on some more credibility. By now, the weeks had turned into months and almost a complete calendar year had gone by and my reports about the story were appearing regularly on my page. Readers had been taken in by it all, just as much as I had been. But then, I allowed a doubt to slip in to one of my stories about the alleged incident, and it wasn't long before I received a letter with a Torquay address from someone, who told me quite categorically that it really had happened and I should not even question it.

The address didn't seem to be quite right, so on the spur of the moment, I rang the newspaper office in Torquay - which was part of our group - and checked it out. There was no such address.

By now the truth was slowly and painfully

beginning to dawn on me. All the letters must have been written and posted by the hoaxer, either when he went off on day trips to nearby places like Doncaster or Nottingham or on holiday to Torquay.

My fears were confirmed, when I had a phone call from someone living on the edge of Nottingham, and he later backed it up with a full letter, which checked out, assuring me the whole thing was a hoax because he knew the man responsible.

The Echo in general, and me in particular, had been well and truly hoaxed, but what on earth the man had gained by it all, will probably remain a mystery for ever. After that incident, I was even more careful about accepting things on face value from people I didn't know. But sometimes, in the high-speed world of newspapers, you do - as I remarked earlier - have to accept some things in all good faith.

Chapter Four

Were Our Faces Red!

Isn't it a shame, isn't it a tragedy that every day of the week and every week of the year, newspapers all over the country get millions and millions of things RIGHT. But we don't remember that. Oh no. We remember the things they get WRONG. The stories, where they have become a complete and utter nonsense through the omission of one word, one letter or even just one punctuation mark.

Or the stories where the headlines have had these dodgy double meanings that nobody has realised until it was too late.

But if you were a regular reader of the Lincolnshire Echo during my 40 years there, you would probably have insisted: "We never saw any printing errors in the Lincolnshire Echo!"

Or then again, perhaps you wouldn't. Perhaps, more correctly, you would have wondered why in that day and age, when we had a multi-million pound brick palace tottering on the brink of Brayford Pool; when we had a multitude of satellite dishes scattered all over the office roof; instant communication to any part of the universe (we couldn't get Channel Five!), why the printing errors were still creeping in?

Well, despite the modern technology, mercifully we still had to employ a few people. People were only human and humans made mistakes. It was just that when we did it, they were there for all to see and to be quoted on occasions such as this.

Because, over the years, I built up my own little black museum of newspaper cuttings with these unfortunate printing errors or headlines and if I may I should like to share some of them with you now.

But this must go no further.

For many years, firmly glued to the wall above my desk, was a wartime headline which proudly announced: "General Montgomery flies back to front."

Then there was a report of a council debate which was headlined: "First motion passed in new chamber." Why was it that everybody else seemed to get that one before I did?

There was a time when the Echo had been guilty of re-naming the RSPB "The Royal Society for The Prevention of Birds." Lincoln Symphony Orchestra was transformed into "The Lincoln Sympathy Orchestra." The Archdeacon became "The Archdemon." A county tenor was horrified the day we described him as "that well-known county terror." The Echo's Bride of the Year once became the Echo's "Bridge of the Year." MI5 became the M15, and that classic war-time film "Ill Met By Moonlight" became "111 Met By Moonlight."

But the one that once got us on the Esther Rantzen That's Life television programme more than 25 years ago, (and what a tragedy they ever took that programme off), was very unfortunate and all we did was to omit one letter from the end of one four-letter word.

The story was all about the Dean of Lincoln, in those days the Very Reverend Oliver Fiennes, who had gone off to Australia with the city's coveted copy of the Magna Carter on a fund-raising mission. Now, towards the end of the story, it should have read: "The

Dean of Lincoln took time off to go to New Zealand for a week."

That's what it should have said. Unfortunately, one letter was left off the end of that last word, and it was all very inconvenient - especially when we said he had done it under the auspicies of the British Tourist Authority. And that got us on to the That's Life television programme.

But the one I suspect they still talk about in hushed terms at the Lincoln Police Headquarters happened some years prior to that.

Now, thank goodness, Lincoln has never been the sort of place to have a reputation for serious crime. But the day eventually arrived, when the city had what was, in all probability, its first murder for years. The police hunt was speedy and successful and it wasn't long before the Chief Constable, a well-respected gentleman called Felix Sayer, held a press conference at four o'clock in the afternoon to announce that a man had been arrested and charged with this dreadful murder.

Four o'clock in the afternoon was not a good time for the Echo. By then most of the papers had been printed, sent off to the newsagents and sold but it was such an important story, that they had to get it in print straight away. And the only way they could do this was by using a Late News column on the back page. On a normal day, it would perhaps contain nothing more dramatic than the afternoon racing results or the half-time soccer scores.

This story was written and printed in haste and when things are done in haste error creeps in. But not on this occasion. It didn't just creep in. Oh no. It galloped in to a fanfare of trumpets.

The story should have read: "The Chief Constable

of Lincoln announced this afternoon that a man has been arrested and charged with murder." That's what it should have said. Unfortunately, some words were left out, and it actually appeared in print as: "The Chief Constable of Lincoln has been arrested and charged with murder."

Yes, it really did. As soon as the mistake was discovered, all hell... I mean a terrible commotion broke out. People were sent off to the newsagents to bring the papers back again quickly and destroy them. But some were sold by a man outside the Stonebow in Lincoln High Street and if, to this very day, you know someone who has got a yellowing copy of the Lincolnshire Echo for 1960 something, get them to look on the back page. If that story is there, I am told they are going up in value all the time.

Slightly more recently, on a Saturday night, the Echo announced to the world that the Ronald Reagan/ Mikhail Gorbachev summit on nuclear disarmament was about to be held in... Washingborough!

All right, so we meant Washington but it actually appeared as Washingborough, which is a fairly large and attractive village just a few miles away from Lincoln, and Washington (of course) isn't.

Obviously it couldn't have been held in Washingborough, because the Community Centre was fully booked that weekend, and there was a do on at the chapel so you would never have parked. But the landlord at the Ferry Boat pub in the village got a crate load of Vodka in, just to be on the safe side.

Some years ago we had a wonderful clergyman in Lincoln, called Canon Ozzie Jones. He was Vicar at St. Mark's Church, a large and impressive stone building, which stood for decades on the corner of High Street, near to the city centre. And he was such a popular preacher that, if you hadn't arrived at his church half an hour before he started on many a Sunday evening, then in all probability you wouldn't have got a seat. He used to fill that place.

Some time in the 1960s, Ozzie told me this story and I am quite sure he wouldn't have made it up. It was all about the Bishop of Grimsby and the Echo's sister newspaper, the Grimsby Evening Telegraph.

The Bishop was booked to give two after-dinner speeches on consecutive evenings. The first night he was in Grimsby and the next night he was three miles down the road at Cleethorpes doing exactly the same thing.

When he was writing his notes in advance he thought, well to save time, he would tell the same jokes each evening and trust to luck that the same people wouldn't be in the audience two nights running.

So, the first night, the Bishop went to Grimsby, he had his meal, rose to his feet, gave his address, told his jokes and sat down. And he thought: "I have got away with it."

Then he noticed sitting at the end of one of the tables was a reporter from the Grimsby Evening Telegraph, who had been taking everything down in shorthand obviously going to do a story for the next day's paper. So the Bishop thought he had better do something about this and when no one was looking he sidled over... No he didn't. Bishop's don't sidle. He walked gracefully over to the reporter and he explained the situation. He said: "Now please feel free to use anything you like from my little talk this evening but would you do me a great favour. Would

44

you leave out the funny stories, because I am telling them again tomorrow night in Cleethorpes and I am dreadfully afraid that if people read them in your paper first, they may not laugh a second time."

So the reporter said: "No problem, my Lord, leave it to me."

Imagine how the Bishop felt the next night, when he opened his copy of the Grimsby Evening Telegraph and he read: "After the dinner the Bishop of Grimsby told some amusing stories... which we are unable to publish."

If I ever find out that story is not true, I shall be so very disappointed.

When I was just starting out at the Echo, we had a senior reporter who was an inveterate chain smoker. I would swear that sometimes you saw him with as many as three cigarettes on the go at the same time - one in his mouth, one in his hand and one behind his ear!

Now this was fine when he was working in the office, because in those days most of the other reporters smoked as well and nobody had really given very much thought to the term "passive smoking".

His trouble really started once he left the office to cover council meetings or courts, because it was absolutely forbidden, of course, to smoke in the hallowed council chamber of the Guildhall or in the dignified surroundings of the Sessions House. And one day, his passion for smoking really got him, and the Echo, into a lot of bother.

He was covering a very lengthy and boring shoplifting case at the magistrates court. A lady was accused of stealing from one of the city centre supermarkets and the police inspector began outlining the case to the magistrates and he went on and he went on and he went on...

After about half-an-hour, the reporter was getting frantic. He desperately needed a cigarette. He started chewing his pen top, he started chewing his notebook and he was about to start taking huge chunks out of the side of the table, when the police inspector finally sat down and the trial began.

The reporter thought, now's my chance. They are going to start going through the evidence and I have already got a note of that in my book. So he slipped quietly out of the courtroom and into the lobby where, out of sight of the magistrates he had one cigarette, he had two and then he had three.

Feeling a lot better, he went back into the courtroom, just in time to hear the chairman of the bench, passing sentence. So he quickly took a note of it, went back to the office and wrote his story.

Now, it wasn't until the story appeared in print the next day and the angry phone calls started coming in, that he realised what had happened. Within moments of the reporter leaving the court for his cigarettes, the chairman of the magistrates had, for some reason or another, decided to adjourn that case to a later date.

They had then started dealing with another, totally different case, involving another woman defendant - who, to be charitable, may perhaps have borne something of a passing resemblance to the first defendant. Then the reporter had come back into court just in time for the end of that case. So what he had done, without realising it, he had tagged the end of that case onto the start of the earlier case.

All that took a lot of explaining away and it does go to show that when you are covering something like the magistrates court, you can't really afford to leave it even for a few minutes, without running the risk of missing something very important.

Now all the other stories I shall recount in these pages are true. I know they are true, either from my own knowledge or because someone I knew and trusted had assured me of their accuracy.

The next one I can't entirely vouch for its accuracy but because it is very much a part of the Echo's living legend, I really ought to include it. You may or may not remember that some years ago, the Archbishop of Canterbury was a lovely gentleman called Doctor Michael Ramsey. And in Lincolnshire we were particularly proud of him because he had a county connection.

In the earlier years of his ministry, he had worked at Lincoln Theological College and I think he was also based in the south of the diocese at some time or other.

Anyway, in his latter years, whenever the Archbishop had a few days to spare, you would quite often find him in Lincoln. He stayed with friends at the Theological College and he would wander round the cathedral quarter chatting informally to the shoppers and everybody loved him.

Well, the time was coming when he was approaching his retirement, and one day the Echo news editor had a little think and it occurred to him that the next time Dr Ramsey visited Lincoln, it could be the last time he would be in the city as archbishop.

So we ought to get someone along to the theological college and do a nice face to face interview with him and see him off in style, he thought. So that's what he arranged to do.

Now the reporter, who was assigned to do this very important interview, hadn't been with the Echo very long. But the news editor thought, well as one of her regular jobs was to write the Churches Page, she was really the reporter for the job.

So she got her notebook and her pen and she set off for the college. When she got there, she was amazed. These were no officials waiting to greet her. No security. No red tape. Nothing. She rang the door bell and the Archbishop himself let her in. She couldn't believe it and she was completely lost for words.

He led her down a corridor and they reached this very comfortable sitting room at the end. There were armchairs, a coffee table, silver tray, cups and saucers, plates of biscuits... Everything was done to make the reporter feel at ease. But right from the start the interview did not go well and the big problem was that the reporter didn't know how to address an archbishop.

I mean, in all fairness, we don't see many of them do we. She started by calling him "sir," which didn't sound right. Then she called him "Your Honour," and that didn't sound any better. So then she tried: "Your Archbishopric," and that was even worse.

So in the end, to get her over the embarrassment, the Archbishop leaned forward in his chair, and passed the plate of biscuits over to her. As he did so, he murmured: "Oh, by the way," and he pointed to himself, "most people will say 'Your Grace'."

Yes, and, as she took a chocolate digestive, she was heard to whisper: "For what we are about to receive..."

Now, I have gone on at some length about my friends and colleagues putting their collective feet into it. Never let it be supposed that in 44 years in newspapers in Lincoln, I have not put my own size seven-and-a-halves into it, just as much as everybody else.

The first time was when I was a very young reporter at the Chronicle. It was the summer and our one and only photographer had gone off on his holidays for a couple of weeks. Now because we couldn't publish an entire newspaper without any pictures and I suppose funds were a bit too tight to set on a relief photographer, the Editor decided to let one of my young colleagues and myself loose with the camera.

To me it was a huge responsibility and I was anxious to use the opportunity to make a bit of a name for myself. At the start of the week I was walking by the cathedral and I glanced up - like you do - and noticed these three men, on a temporary wooden platform roughly the size of a snooker table, busy repairing a stone cross high up on the roof.

In my childish innocence, a crazy idea began to form in my mind. "Wouldn't it be good," I thought, "if I could go up onto the roof and take a picture of those three men at work. I would be famous."

So I went back to the office, which we shared with the local Liberal Club, and rang the Subdean, who I had got to know reasonably well through regular stories about the need to raise money for the cathedral repairs and I explained what I wanted to do.

He was always helpful, and he said I could go along the next day and he would meet me outside the cathedral and show me the best way to the top.

In those days you have to bear in mind that the newspaper cameras were still very primitive. We didn't have any of these digital things. We didn't have discs and we didn't even use rolls of film. We had glass negative plates, roughly the size of a small postcard and before going off on a job, in the gloom of the darkroom, you had to put each glass negative plate from one pile, into a metal container from another pile.

If you had about 20 of them in your camera bag, along with the heavy camera, the whole thing seemed to weigh a ton and a half.

Having loaded my camera bag, I set off to climb up the local mountain which we call Steep Hill, to the cathedral where the Subdean was waiting for me. Now, if you ever decide to go to the top of Lincoln Cathedral - and it is well worth the trip - you will discover that part of the journey is fairly easy. It's inside, through a succession of spiral staircases and narrow passageways.

Then there comes a time, when it becomes just a little bit more challenging. You have to go outside. We reached this point. I was gasping for breath, having struggled up something like 300 stone steps with this heavy camera bag over my shoulder.

As we stepped out into the sunlight, high above the ground, the Subdean pointed into the sky and said: "That's where you want to be."

For one moment, I thought he was pointing to heaven. Then I realised there was a vertical ladder going up from where we were to this platform surrounding that stone cross. There were three men on the platform, and from that distance, it looked as though they were standing in a passing cloud, it was that far away.

It was at this point the Subdean suddenly remembered he had an appointment back at the Subdeanery, so he disappeared and left me to it. Now, I have got to be honest, I don't like climbing ladders. At home, I used to make my wife clean the windows. But I couldn't go down or I would risk losing face. So I started to climb this ladder, one very slow and very careful rung at a time, and eventually (and I had got to be running out of oxygen by this time) I arrived on this platform and it didn't look as sturdy as it did when I was down on the ground looking up.

There were already three men on this platform, so there was hardly any room for me. They regarded me with something approaching indifference. To me it was a big adventure. To them it was an everyday occurrence and I suspect they regarded me as a bit of a hinderance.

For the next few minutes. I grimly hung on to anything I could find, while trying to take pictures at the same time. In the end, I had taken what I thought were probably enough pictures and I scrambled back down the ladder, a lot faster than I had come up it.

I hurried back to the office. By this time, it was getting fairly late in the day and most of the people had gone home. But there was no way I was going home without seeing these pictures I risked my life and limb to take.

Into the dark room. Lights out. Negatives out of their metal containers, into the developer, into the fixer...

It was not until I started to print the pictures, that I realised what I had done.

In my haste to load the negative plates before setting off, I had inadvertantly taken most of them from a stack of previously-exposed plates. Now you don't need a degree in photography to know that you cannot use the same negative twice. It just doesn't work. No matter what you do, you are still left with the original image.

So when I printed off my pictures, I found that instead of magnificent shots of men repairing the stone cross at the top of the cathedral, I had pictures taken several days earlier, showing coach parties going off to the seaside, weddings, jumble sales, school sports days, birthday parties, the lot.

Only one or two of my cathedral pictures actually came out. But the Editor, out of the kindness of his heart, used one of them on the back page, and from that day, for quite a few years to come, I never had another picture published in any newspaper known to mankind.

Much later on, I was to discover that even the so-called "idiot-proof" cameras couldn't always be relied on.

Came the day I was off to the local commercial television studios to meet the new regional reporter, and I needed a picture to accompany my story about him. There was no Echo photographer around at the time, so I was given this "all new, all singing, all dancing, idiot-proof" camera. There was no film to worry about. I was assured that all I had to do was pick up the camera, point it in the right direction, and press a button.

Well, I did pick up the camera. I did point it in the right direction and I did press the button... only to discover that the battery was dead.

Another cringe-worthy event happened one November, when the Echo, local radio and regional television were all looking back on a rare anniversary. It was forty years to the day since The Beatles had paid their one and only visit to Lincoln.

John, Paul, Ringo and George had once appeared for two memorable sell-out performances on the stage of the old ABC Cinema in Saltergate. The 1,800-seat cinema had staged many big-name pop shows in its history but nobody ever disputed that The Beatles were the biggest of them all. The group hadn't quite reached the peak of their career at that time but with records like Please, Please Me, Love Me Do and She Loves You, they were the group that everybody had wanted to see.

Forty years later, the old ABC had long gone, and as the 20th century drew to a close, the old building was demolished and the site incorporated into a new multi-million pound shopping complex. But with a little bit of local knowledge and a good memory, it was more or less possible to stand at a certain point in the shopping complex and say with a fair degree of accuracy: "This is where the stage used to be and this is where The Beatles would have played."

William Wright, from BBC Radio Lincolnshire, took me down to the shopping centre so I could point out the spot to him. And after he did some interviews with passersby he managed to enlist a small number of attractive young ladies to stand on what would have been the stage, with me, and exactly forty years after The Beatles had done it, we had to sing a few bars of "She Loves You".

I think that's the only occasion when I have ever sung on the radio, and anyone hearing the broadcast would have known why.

When you are interviewing someone, either face to face or on the end of a telephone, there is one question that you really have to ask. You need, if you can, to find the age of the person you are talking to. It's a very relevant and important piece of information, particularly on the telephone when you sometimes haven't a clue if the person on the other end of the line is young with an elderly-sounding voice or an elderly person with a young voice.

You just can't tell. But it is a very embarrassing question to ask because some people, quite correctly, don't like talking about their age. So over the years. I found a way of wrapping up this very important question in such a way that I hoped didn't offend or embarrass the person I was talking to.

So what I would do, at some convenient time in the conversation, I would put on my most innocent expression and say: "Can I be very rude, and ask how old you are?"

And if the person was going to tell you, they would and if they didn't want to, well we would go on to talk about something else and I just hoped I hadn't offended them. So that's what I would do. I would say: "Can I be very rude and ask how old you are?"

Until the day I was doing a lengthy telephone interview with a man who lived not far from Boston. His main hobby was making model steam engines, and I believe he was very good at it as well. And I really needed to know how old he was, because I suspected he may be some very impressive age.

I was all set to ask: "Can I be very rude and ask how old you are?" But what I actually said to him was: "Can I be very old and ask how rude you are?"

Yes, I did and the worst part about it was that I knew I was going to say it. Everybody within earshot fell about laughing and I had to have an attack of coughing to get over that. To this day, I still dread asking that question.

Chapter Five

The High-Flying Bishop

Towards the end of my career at the Echo, I was involved in perhaps the most audacious thing I have ever done. Now, one of my greatest loves, in addition to circuses, steam engines and newspapers, is the fairground. Through my part-time work as a correspondent for the national showmen's newspaper, World's Fair, I travel to anything between 50 and 100 fairs during the course of the season, and over the years I have made some excellent contacts and built up some wonderful friendships among the fairground folk.

Whenever I had the opportunity to write Echo stories, which were going to help promote the county's fairs, I was more than happy to do so.

Now, in the early part of this century, the fairs at Lincoln were going through perhaps one of their most difficult periods in recent history. For one reason or another, the public just weren't supporting them in the way they once had and the city council eventually announced it could no longer afford to go on staging the twice-yearly fairs on the South Common.

The fairs would almost certainly have disappeared completely, if it hadn't been for the Showmen's Guild, which, at short notice, stepped in and took control of the events so the ancient tradition wouldn't be lost.

But finance was tight and the Guild didn't have a lot of money to spend on publicity, so one of the leading figures on the fairground, William Wood, came up with an idea, which he hoped would attract some free publicity.

It was the September Fair of 2005, and included among the line-up of attractions for the first time in Lincoln was something called the Reverse Bungee. Intrepid riders were securely fastened into a two-person device which catapulted them 200 feet into the air, and after a series of breath-taking bounces, they were lowered back to the ground again.

Could I think of a local celebrity who might be prepared to be catapulted 200 feet into the air to raise £1,000 for charity? That was the question William asked me, as the fair was preparing to open. And my mind immediately turned to the Bishop of Lincoln, the Right Reverend John Saxbee, who since he had arrived in the diocese not so long ago, had endeared himself to churchgoers and non-churchgoers alike by doing a free-fall parachute jump to help a good cause.

He was also planning a flight with the Lincolnshire-based Red Arrows aerobatic team, so I had no doubt at all that being catapulted 200 feet into the air was quite within his capabilities.

But how do you invite a Bishop to do something like that? We had never met and I didn't want to run the risk of offending him or of him thinking that it was perhaps just a cheap publicity stunt and that his time would be better spent elsewhere.

And we didn't have very many days to play with. Eventually I plucked up courage to ring the Bishop's secretary, and I could hardly have got a more encouraging reply. He had a word with the Bishop, rang me back, and within the next day or so William and I had arrived at the Bishop's house in the shadow of the cathedral and were explaining exactly what we wanted.

The Bishop couldn't have been more helpful. He

offered to be at the fair at eight o'clock at night - which was ideal from everyone's point of view because by then there would be plenty of people at the fair to give him their support. He even volunteered to wear his cloak and his cross around his neck, for the benefit of the photographers and television cameramen.

He arrived on the South Common and met by some of the showmen and I, he walked between the rides and stalls, looking perfectly relaxed and happy about the whole thing. He didn't even flinch when he stood at the base of the two mighty towers and looked up into the night sky at where he was about to go.

William had been to the bank earlier in the day and had £1,000 in notes to hand him once the Bishop was safely back on earth.

There had been just one little doubt which had been niggling me since I got involved in the stunt and that was just who would accompany the Bishop on the ride. I had made it abundantly clear from the start that it wouldn't be me. While I might be mad, I am certainly not crazy and there was no way I was going to be catapulted 200 feet into the night sky - even with a Bishop for company.

In the end, my worries were settled when one of the showladies, who was celebrating her 45th birthday, volunteered to accompany him.

There was an impressive gasp of breath from the watching crowd and the television camera crew, as the Bishop and his fellow traveller vanished briefly into the night sky, before they came bouncing back down again, to cheers and applause.

And I shall never forget the Bishop's words, when he first agreed to take part: "By and large, Bishops are keen to spend a lot of their time with an eye to heaven. This may be an opportunity for me to get a closer look."

I have no doubt that it did.

Working for a provincial newspaper doesn't give you many opportunities of foreign travel, so on the odd occasion when overseas trips have become available, I have grasped them warmly with both hands.

The first must have been in the early 1990s, in the days when the Echo was promoting a lot of reader holidays. I spotted we were advertising a coach trip to Czechoslovakia and thought it sounded a bit different. And the price was amazing too. Admittedly there was overnight travel but once you got there it was full board in a good quality hotel. I looked at the price and I looked at what was on offer, and for the life of me I just couldn't see where the profit came from.

It almost looked too good to be true and it was even better for me because when I asked about two tickets for the trip, I was told that if I wanted to act as the courier, I could travel free. Now, I had never been a courier in my life but spurred on by the thought that nothing could really go very wrong, I eagerly agreed.

It was February and there was snow on the ground as we boarded the coach outside the Echo office and I remember giving some encouraging welcoming speech to my fellow travellers about how it wasn't going to be so much of a holiday as an adventure. Because, at the time, the barriers had only recently come down and Czechoslovakia was only just beginning to welcome foreign tourists in a big way.

We set off and despite the weather and lack of sleep, we duly arrived at the German border. I seem to remember everyone giving a little cheer as the coach halted briefly at customs and carried on into what had previously been "no man's land" leading up to the Czech frontier. But the cheers came to an abrupt end, as the coach came to an unscheduled halt again and we discovered we had broken down yards short of our destination.

The coach needed a spare part and it seemed the nearest one was at Walsall in the Midlands - hundreds of miles away from were we now were. But somehow, I think thanks to the driver's ingenuity, we managed to get going again and arrived at our hotel. The spare part arrived by air the next day.

I suspect that the cost of living in what used to be Czechoslovakia has risen considerably since our visit, because at the time we couldn't believe just how cheap it was. We had become millionaires overnight.

We discovered we could walk into even the most fashionable restaurant in Prague and order anything we liked from the menu without bothering to look at the prices, because we knew we could pay for even the most expensive meal out of our loose change. It was the only time in my life when I have felt really rich.

Whenever our coach stopped for any length of time, a small crowd of locals would gather round to take a closer look. But it wasn't the television, the drinks dispenser or the fact there was a toilet on board that seemed to impress them. They couldn't get over the fact, the driver had a telephone.

Across the road from our hotel was a little shop which had a fine selection of crockery in its window, and almost every day, one of the ladies in our party would wander over to the shop to take a closer look. On the last day, she counted up her remaining money and decided that, yes, she really could afford that very nice plate in the window. It was perhaps just a little bit more than she would have paid for a plate in England but she had enjoyed her holiday so much and she wanted a nice souvenir to take home with her.

The shopkeeper was delighted and so was our passenger, especially when she realised that for the money she was paying she wasn't just getting a single plate. She was getting an entire dinner service, which was such an excellent quality that it took two men to carry it back to the coach.

My last taste of foreign travel, before I was to bid a fond farewell to the Echo, had to be one of the highlights of my career as a journalist - and yet I doubt if it would ever have come about if it hadn't been for my part-time job as a clown.

By the early months of 2004, I suppose I had become a fairly familiar face around the corridors of the BBC Radio Lincolnshire headquarters at the old Radion Cinema in Lincoln. I was being featured almost every week on Melvyn Prior's Saturday lunchtime show, generally on nostalgic matters and four or five times a year on the Treasure Trove spot on a Saturday morning.

There was no money involved but the management at the Echo were quite happy for me to do it because it helped, in a small way, to promote not just The Gossiper column but the Lincolnshire Echo as a whole.

Radio Lincolnshire supports a good cause every year, and in 2004 they had decided to raise money for the Wish Upon A Star charity and if they raised enough by the end of the year, they hoped to fly 100 desperately ill children, along with their parents and a team of helpers and medical personnel, to Lapland for the day to meet "the real Santa Claus". They were onto a winner right from the start, because it was a charity that clearly touched people's hearts straight away and the money poured in as never before.

I couldn't believe it when the people at Radio Lincolnshire asked if I would be willing to go on the flight in a dual capacity - first as an Echo representative, taking pictures on the aircraft and in Lapland, and second in the guise of Pedro the Clown, helping to entertain the children before, during and after the trip.

As I recall, I didn't need a lot of persuasion. It was the opportunity of a lifetime, although I did have to take a long, hard look at a World Atlas before I could even be sure just where Lapland was. If I had ever thought about Lapland before, I suppose I had always pictured it as being somewhere near Greenland or Iceland and I was a bit surprised when I discovered it was actually at the top of Finland. Although, to put it in prospective, it's on the Arctic Circle and even further north than Iceland and parts of Greenland.

I had plenty of time to prepare for the trip and plenty of time to worry about it as well, because I was being relied on by both the Echo and Radio Lincolnshire, to come up with some pretty good pictures, and bearing in mind my track record on the photographic front, you could see why I was just a little bit worried.

And even if the Echo's idiot-proof camera really did manage to live up to its name on the trip, there was no guarantee that it would function at all in the bitterly cold temperatures of a December day in the Arctic.

Television personality Jeremy Spake, who had

done the trip before on a number of occasions and was accompanying us on this adventure, told me with a sort of fiendish delight, that it was possible the temperatures could be as low as minus 28 degrees once we stepped out of the aircraft.

By now, I was genuinely worried, so I consulted the only photographer I knew who had ever worked in those kinds of temperatures, the globe-trotting Mike Maloney, who comes from Lincoln and has won more photographic awards than possibly any other national photographer in history. He gave me some valuable tips, which as it turned out, I didn't really need because when we got to Lapland, they were having one of their mildest December days for years. Three cheers for global warming!

Because we had a very early start from Nottingham East Midlands Airport, most of us stayed the previous night at a hotel a few minutes drive away and there was a reception the night before in which I donned my Pedro the Clown costume and mingled with the parents and children, trying to put them and myself at ease. An Echo photographer was at the reception as well, getting some picture just in case the ones I took in Lapland didn't come out.

I didn't get a lot of sleep that night - not because I wasn't in bed early,but because I had to be up at three in the morning to put my clown make-up on and my costume and get down into the hotel lobby to greet everyone as they staggered out of the lift, bleary-eyed, and stumbled off in the direction of breakfast before leaving for the airport and I didn't want to be late.

It was going to be a very long day but one I would never forget.

Getting through the airport check-in and waiting around in the lounge until we could board the chartered aircraft seemed to take an eternity and I was still in clown costume as the Boeing 757 soared into the air just before half past seven.

Since I first started to juggle, one question has often cropped up in my mind: Is it possible to juggle on an aircraft in flight? Well, yes it is, because I did it that day. It must be something like a clown's equivalent to the Mile High Club, because I can now boast that I have juggled three bean bags at 36,000 feet while travelling at something like 500 mph.

The fact that I didn't use my juggling clubs was purely and simply because you don't get a lot of room in the aisle between the seats, and every time I took a few steps in either direction, during the three-hour flight, I had to stop because there was always someone coming the other way.

As we walked through the customs at Roveneimi Airport, I got a very strange look from the man who checked the passports, because my face in clown make-up looks nothing like it does on my passport picture. But after signing a slip of paper, I was allowed to join the rest of the party, rapidly putting on winter thermals and boots for our first taste of an Arctic winter.

It may not have been particularly cold but there was plenty of snow around as we left the airport - which doubles as a civilian airfield and a military base - and boarded our coaches for a trip through pine forests and along snow-covered roads. If we had encountered that sort of weather here in Britain, the police would have been telling everyone not to travel, most of the schools would have been closed and the television would have been putting out severe weather warnings. But in the Arctic, life seems to carry on as normal.

The only thing that worried me, from a photographic point of view, was that there didn't seem to be a lot of daylight. Back home my colleagues at the Echo office would have been trying to slip out to snatch a bite or two of lunch but up here in Lapland, the long, dark night was already beginning to set in.

We stopped in a clearing in a snow-covered forest, where the children, and one or two of the adults as well, enjoyed rides on sledges drawn by reindeer and by dogs. There was plenty of warm drinks and hot food, and although we were all standing around in deep snow, it didn't seem particularly cold.

Before we all boarded the coaches again, the locals had even laid on a firework display for us and that made the whole thing even more magical. Our next stop was in a reasonably large town where Jeremy took great delight in pointing out to us the world's most northerly McDonalds. It seems that no matter where you happen to be on the planet, you just can't escape them.

In a warm hotel, alongside a river, which was frozen solid, the children met "the real Santa Claus", and I must admit he really did look the part. And he spoke English too, which was a great benefit to us all.

Afterwards, while the party was going on, I slipped back to the coach, which was parked at the front of the hotel, and - with the aid of a mobile phone provided by the Echo specially for the occasion - I telephoned my story back to a copytypist in the Lincoln office. Isn't modern technology a wonderful thing! It seemed really strange, sitting in a dimly-lit coach, dictating a story, surrounded by ice and snow, with the occasional reindeer wandering by and knowing that back in the office life would be going on as it did on any other Friday afternoon.

Our next stop was at Santa's Village, which is an amazing place right on the Arctic Circle itself. By now it was well dark and getting late in the afternoon but the village was well worth exploring and I went in Santa's Post Office, admired the ice sculptures outside and even had an ice cream while standing in the snow.

It was well into the evening by the time we arrived back at the airport and there were the inevitable queues while we waited to board the plane. I would guess that by this time just about every adult in the party was flagging. When, clearly audible from the back of the queue, was this very excited, very ill, little girl who was jumping up and down, singing Jingle Bells very loudly and very out of tune.

I think, to me, that summed up the entire experience. I hope one day to be able to afford to go back again with my family but even if I do it will never be quite the same.

Oh and yes, for once my pictures did come out.

Chapter Six

Unaccustomed As I Am

Have you ever been asked to make a speech? No, I don't mean standing up in front of your family and friends at a wedding, and making a complete and utter fool of yourself as you struggle to remember whether your maiden aunt bought you the duvet or the dinner service. But the sort of speech which is designed to illustrated that you know at least more than the basic elements about your job, and that you can describe it in a way which is going to be coherent and vaguely interesting.

I hadn't been at the Lincolnshire Echo for very long, before I was starting to get invitations from organisations to go along and give them a talk all about my work. It didn't take me a great length of time to realise that the requests generally came from some far flung part of the circulation area, or they were to attend meetings which seemed to take place at night, or at inconvenient times, or they were in a part of the city where there was some sort of local controversy going on.

At first I must admit I felt just a little bit flattered that complete strangers should feel inclined to invite me, a perfect stranger, along to one of their meetings to address them. Then, niggling doubts began to creep in. My name wasn't appearing regularly in the newspaper, as this was all in my pre-Gossiper days. So why were all these people suddenly wanting me to go along and talk to them?

Then the truth began to dawn on me. The requests

were originally being made to my far more knowledgeable colleagues who were all very familiar with the perils of public speaking, and they were passing on my name as an easy way out.

After successfully avoiding the first few, I eventually bowed to pressure and agreed to go along to a meeting which seemed to be composed almost entirely of ladies. The title of my so-called talk was something vague like "My Job", and I think I must have written almost every word out in advance, and just stood in front of the audience and read it over to them. Looking back, they must have been as bored as I was, as I religiously took them through almost every minute of the typical working day (if there really is such a thing in journalism) describing in great detail what went in to producing a newspaper week in week out.

I can't deny that I enjoyed my work, but the last thing I really wanted to do after a hard eight-hour shift, was scrambling home for a few minutes, grabbing a bite to eat, having to get changed into my best suit, and driving off into the night to talk to sometimes a handful of people in a chilly village hall at the other end of the county.

One evening, I think it must have been out of sheer desperation, I ventured to put a little joke in at the end of my talk, and people were kind enough to laugh. So I thought, well hang on a minute. Let's re-write the speech in what I hoped would be a humorous way, getting over most of what I wanted to say, but telling a few related jokes along the way.

I reasoned that if I was going to do these talks regularly, I might as well have a go at enjoying them, or I would be sentencing myself to years and years of misery.

Then, I went really, really brave. What if, at the end of my talk, I suddenly took off my jacket, my tie and my shirt, and juggled with three fire torches? It may not bear any relationship to what I had been talking about, but I was pretty sure there were no other speakers in the county who did anything similar and it would give me a very different finish to the evening.

By now, I had given my talk the "amusingly witty" title: A Funny Kind of Evening with The Gossiper. I would have my notes secured to a clip board, which would give me something to do with my left hand, and I had a pen in my right hand, which I would move around for effect.

Later on, in the fullness of time, I would use a mobile phone to illustrate telephone calls which had played an important part in my life.

I was beginning to feel more and more comfortable facing an audience, and I found I needed to refer to my notes less and less. So I kept the clipboard only for when it appeared as if I wanted to refer to something someone had said, or something which had been published, word for word.

It didn't take me long to realise that I couldn't use my fire torches at every venue. Sometimes the ceiling was far too low. Sometimes the room was much too small. There would be times when the front row of the audience was much too near for safety. Occasionally there would be billowing curtains uncomfortably close.

Then there were the "no smoking" signs on the wall. Many a time I had to grapple with my conscience about those. Did they apply merely to cigarettes, cigars and pipes, or did they mean fire torches as well?

Although I didn't decide until I was actually in

the room, whether or not to use the fire torches, I had to dowse them with paraffin in the car park outside, just in case I could use them. And many a time, the audience's noses much have twitched as I entered the room, accompanied by that very distinctive smell of paraffin.

The torches would be concealed inside a brief case or a modest little canvas bag, which I would place prominently on the table, where it could be easily seen by everybody. At the start, I would hint that there was something in the bag, which people might find vaguely amusing, and if there was time at the end of the talk, I would open the bag and show them.

If the room wasn't suitable, I would quietly slip the bag under my chair and make no reference to it.

Usually, during the vote of thanks at the end of the talk, someone would mention the bag, and ask if I would open it, and I would rise to my feet with the words: "When people were first kind enough to invite me to attend their meetings, I quickly realised that I was at a bit of disadvantage because I didn't do anything.

"I mean, I don't demonstrate flower arranging, I don't show slides. I don't show films. It's just me standing here - for hour after hour - talking. So I thought, what can I show you that you may not have seen before?"

At this point I would take off my jacket.

"Is there a little something...?"

By now, my tie would be off and I would have started unbuttoning my shirt. At this point, some of the ladies in the front row would be laughing, others would be looking uncomfortable, and you didn't have to be any sort of mindreader to imagine the thoughts that were running through their heads. They must have considered I was raving mad.

And I would go on: "Then I thought it does give me a chance to show you my little hobby."

By now my shirt would be off, and most of the audience would be laughing. Why was it that at this point, many of the ladies would be taking a sidelong glance to gauge the reaction of the woman who always turned out to be the wife of the local vicar?

Then I would reach into my bag, bring out the three torches, one at a time, and hand them to people sitting on the front row. I would ask them to hold the torches while I lit them, washing my hands in the flames and pretending to get burned, and then suggesting that as the Olympics were approaching, the three ladies might like to have a little race around the village, holding a fire torch in their hands.

At this point, the room would be filling with the smoke from the torches, and some people would be starting to cough and wondering if they could quietly open a window without drawing too much attention to themselves.

So, fairly quickly, I would take hold of the fire torches and juggle with them for a few moments, before blowing them out and sitting down, to what was usually a reasonable round of applause.

All went well, until I was giving a talk at a village hall in a place called Saxilby, not far from Lincoln. By this time, I had done the fire torches piece of the talk more than a hundred times, spanning a number of years, so I was feeling very relaxed and complacent about the whole thing.

I had juggled with the fire torches in the same hall, when I had talked to a different organisation just a few weeks earlier, so the venue held no fears for me. There was a high ceiling and plenty of room.

What they hadn't told me, and what I hadn't realised, was that between my visits, someone had installed a very efficient smoke alarm in the hall.

I had just lit my third fire torch and was about to start to juggle with them, when the alarm went off. There was this terrible noise and a blue light started flashing on the wall outside.

Now, I don't know whether this is general or not when it comes to smoke alarms, but once this one sounded, there didn't seem to be an easy way of turning it off again. So I am frantically running around the hall, stripped to the waist, in the middle of January, desperately trying to find a way to turn this thing off.

What you may not know is that the hall at Saxilby, is located very close to the village fire station, and I had visions that it wouldn't be very long before the local fire brigade arrived and began smashing their way into the room with axes, intent on rescuing everyone inside.

To this day, I am not entirely sure whether it was something I did or someone else did something, that stopped the alarm in the nick of time, but I can assure you that ever since then, I have scanned the ceilings very carefully for any sign of a smoke detector before lighting up my fire torches.

Sometimes when you are addressing a meeting, you fall into the trap of thinking that everybody can hear every word you say, and understands it perfectly. But it isn't necessarily so.

I was giving a talk one afternoon to a Women's Institute not far from Sleaford. Now, Women's Institutes are probably my favourite audience, because the meetings are quite often well attended by ladies who are intent on having a good time and seem to enjoy a bit of a laugh.

And this particular afternoon was, thankfully, no exception. Afterwards, I was talking to the chairman who told me proudly that on the front row were two ladies well into their nineties, who still regularly attended the meetings.

So I thought I had better go over to them and have a word. As I approached, one of them said to me: "Now then young man (I warmed to her immediately), and where do you come from?"

I smiled, what I hoped would be interpreted as my warmest smile, and replied: "Born and bred in Lincoln."

The expression on her face never changed. "Pardon?" she asked.

I raised my voice slightly, while smiling at the same time, and that isn't as easy to do as you might think.

"Born and bred in Lincoln!" I repeated.

The lady's expression still didn't change, and I realised she still hadn't heard me. After four or five attempts I was almost screaming at the top of my voice: "Born and bred in Lincoln!"

At last, a look of acknowledgement began to spread across her face. I had got through at last, or I had thought I had.

"Oh, I like Bournemouth!" she said.

I gave up, and we spent the next few minutes having a very audible conversation about joys and benefits of the south coast.

Most of the village and church halls you visit are well lit and comfortable and some of them are really spectacular - like one in a Nottinghamshire village not far from Ollerton, where they have very tastefully converted the old parish church and another in a small village not far from Market Rasen where you could be forgiven for thinking you are standing in the well-appointed drawing room of an old manor house.

On the face of it, one of the halls I went to in North Hykeham - a town which borders onto Lincoln - looked well equipped with just about everything you might have expected it to have. But on the occasion of my visit it didn't have electricity - at least, not in the main room.

The power had failed and the only light we had was the eerie glow from the emergency exit signs about the doors, and a light shining in from the kitchen. But we soldiered on and I was only grateful that by then I had learned my talk almost word perfect, as I wouldn't have stood any chance at all of reading anything in what little light we had.

Quite often, towards the end of the meeting, the guest speaker will be invited to judge a competition. I think the organisers try to engineer it so that the topic is something the speaker is likely to know a bit about, so I generally find myself faced with judging the funniest headline, the best newspaper cartoon or the most humorous misprint.

But occasionally I have to venture into whole new realms which I know next to nothing about. I have raved enthusiastically about the best flowers, the best-decorated tea cosy and the most attractively-produced piece of pottery, even if I hadn't really understood what it was all about. But the competition I think I found the most difficult, was having to judge the best jar of homemade jam - without being allowed to taste it.

The only point I felt I could judge it on what just how it looked and that didn't seem to be a great help.

Now, I have got to admit, that I have never been a very great fan of Punch and Judy shows. I don't know why but there you are. I do know that I am probably among a minority of people with this view and you have only got to pause on a seaside beach for any length of time and watch a crowd of excited youngsters screaming their heads off as Mr. Punch falls foul of the policeman or the crocodile to know how very popular they are.

But my dislike (coupled with just a small degree of fear perhaps) may well stem from the time when I was asked to help judge the finals of a national Punch and Judy Competition.

The event was taking place at a holiday camp in Mablethorpe and although it may well have been the middle of summer, I seem to remember the weather left a lot to be desired. It was one of those days when the sky was absolutely full of grey clouds and the wind was driving the rain into your face. There was no question of the competition being held on the beach, so all the booths were moved into the main clubroom.

I say "all", but in truth there weren't a great number, although there were quite enough to those of us who were judging. Also on the panel I remember there was a Yorkshire comedian called Jimmy Marshall, who I had seen on television a few times and he mercifully did his best to stop us all from going mad as one after another the contestants went through their paces.

There was an audience of young children as well, and a couple of television crews were capturing it all for posterity. But after the first two or three versions of the story - which doesn't really change a great deal - I could have quite happily throttled the next little wooden puppet to utter those words "Judy, Judy, Judy."

From everyone's point of view I suppose the competition was a great success. It brought some very good television and press coverage to the Lincolnshire coast in general and to one holiday camp in particular. The Punch and Judy professors had their few minutes of glory, and one of them won a trophy and would no doubt in future bill himself as "Britain's top Punch and Judy Show."

But it left something of a lasting impression on me - and I am sure on the rest of the judging panel as well. And to this day I can't glimpse a Punch and Judy booth in the distance without remembering that day.

But the most memorable competition it was ever my pleasure or challenge to judge, was something they called "The First British Topless Bathing Beauty Contest".

I am sure you couldn't do it nowadays, but at the time you could and they did. It sounds a bit like something from a Carry On film, doesn't it? A gentleman, who later became a very long-standing friend, had the idea and wanted to hold heats of the competition every week at Skegness. But the local council, perhaps fearing something of a backlash from the ladies on the council, shook their heads and said very firmly that the contest couldn't be held in any of their venues.

Undaunted my friend took the idea to a very large privately-run nightspot at nearby Ingoldmells. The idea was there would be half-a-dozen heats and the winner every week would go into the grand final at the end of the season.

He invited me to judge one of the heats and the final. Now the Lincolnshire holiday coast isn't the south of France and it isn't Ibiza. In fact, it's a very long way away from any of those Mediterranean beaches, where the young ladies are quite prepared to whip off their bikini tops and stroll around under the sunshine all day and right from the start it was fairly obvious they were going to have trouble in attracting a large number of entries.

But there were a handful of models and would-be models who saw it as a way of attracting instant nationwide publicity. Surprisingly I don't remember any sort of protests at all about the competition but it was perhaps the most difficult thing I have ever been asked to judge.

My friend told me afterwards, that some of the women in his office had put him under a certain amount of pressure to hold a contest that might appeal to the ladies and a "Mr. Wet Underpants" competition had been put forward. But happily, as far as I am aware, it never got off the ground.

Chapter Seven

Computer Crazy

"You must have seen so many changes during your working life, what are the most memorable?"

I must have asked that question so many times myself, while interviewing men and women who were just about to retire. And inevitably the time came when someone was to ask it of me.

And there were really so many changes that I hardly know where to begin. When I started, the press, where the Echoes were printed six days a week, was very labour intensive. It was a hot, noisy and I suspect far from pleasant place to work. We typed out stories on scraps of paper called copy paper (because the stories we wrote were called 'copy'). They were carefully checked by a sub-editor who wrote a headline on the top, rolled it up and dropped it down a drainpipe-type tube onto the floor below. Here the stories were opened and handed to a linotype operator who copied them out into metal type.

There was one memorable day - I suppose I must have been feeling a little bit bored or something - when I sent down a wad of stories, fastened to the end of a long piece of cotton. When the stories landed at the bottom of the tube, with a satisfying thud, I heard the man downstairs open the little door to retrieve them. But before he could, I pulled on the piece of cotton and whisked the stories back up the chute again.

I would have loved to have seen his face, as the

pieces of paper disappeared from his grasp.

After the stories had been set into metal, an awful lot of things happened to them, which I won't bore you with - largely because I never really did understand what they were or why they happened. But sufficient to say, the re-typed stories were checked against the originals and if everything was in order, pages were made up and eventually the whole paper would be printed.

It was such a good system that you wondered how anything could ever have gone wrong but from time to time it did.

A few decades on, the process had been trimmed down enormously and I am afraid that job losses had been made along the way. Computers had arrived.

Now, the first computer I ever saw was sometime in the 1960s, when one of the local secondary schools gained one and it was enormous. I kid you not, it took up an entire room - and a fairly large room at that. It was some years later before the editorial staff of the Echo were entrusted with them and I must admit I was something of a reluctant entrant into the world of computers.

It all started the day I asked for a new ribbon for the portable typewriter which stood on my desk. I don't know, it would probably have cost no more than a few shillings from Woolworth's. But I didn't get my ribbon. Oh no. The next morning, a man staggered onto the editorial floor carrying this television screen, which must have been something like the size of the Odeon's. I somehow found a space on my desk just large enough to accommodate the computer screen. Now this was no mean achievement in itself, because my desk was never famous for being entirely paper free.

There were so many letters, photographs and files I had accumulated over the years, that they had grown into a little mountain which was close to being shown on Ordnance Survey maps. Right to my final day at the Echo. I always successfully resisted every effort to keep my desk tidy and when ever anyone in authority used to talk about our office being "paper free" I always knew the reference could never be applied to my particular part of it.

Anyway you couldn't deny my computer screen was impressive. You almost expected it to have curtains which would suddenly sweep apart and a man at an electronic organ would rise up from the floor in front of it. There was a keyboard as well which thankfully bore more than a passing resemblance to my more familiar typewriter.

But one thing I never did quite get the hang of was that you don't have to pound the keys in the same way as you did a typewriter.

When it came to training how to use this new monster, I am sure we were all given some very comprehensive and useful hints. But I can't really remember any of them. What I do remember is experts arriving from time to time, sitting straight in front of the screen and hiding the keyboard from view, so there was no way you could ever find out what he had done and how. I had this theory that most of the people who were proficient with a computer, didn't really want to pass on all their knowledge to you, because once they had done, you would have known as much as they did and they would have become redundant.

It was the same with many of the people who came to sort things out when the computers went wrong, as they invariably did. The first line of defence when you rang the IT men, to tell them you had been sitting at your screen for half-an-hour and nothing appeared to be happening was always: "Have you tried switching it off and switching it back on again?" Or: "Are you sure it's plugged in?"

And they had a language all of their own.

"The computers have crashed!"

The first time I heard someone say that I remember anxiously looking up at the ceiling, expecting to see them come tumbling through from the floor above.

And it didn't take me long to realise that most computers - at least all the ones that I ever worked on - had a mind of their own and a very wicked sense of humour. Now, I don't know how familiar you are with computers but somewhere on the keyboard and I have never intentionally found it, is a key that if you happen to press it, has the power to obliterate your morning's work entirely. Or if it doesn't actually obliterate it, then it sends it to some half-forgotten part of the universe and you can never see it again.

One day, when I seemed to be under more pressure than usual and I had just managed to complete a very difficult story, I would swear I didn't even touch the offending key. A passing breeze drifted gently across the room. It wafted across my keyboard. I looked up at the screen, and everything had been sent to oblivion - that black hole, somewhere in infinity, which is gradually being filled up by all the stories which are being accidentally fed to it by people on earth.

Why anyone in their right minds should ever want to invent a key to do such a thing, I could never imagine but if they did then they should at least have had the decency to mark it in red so we could easily distinguish it from all the others.

There were other changes to the newspaper

industry as well which marked my 44 years in journalism. For instance, when I started, the Echo was arguably the only way that the people of large parts of Lincolnshire, got their news. There was some regional television but a local news item had to be pretty major before it would find its way onto TV.

Free sheets were perhaps the first serious competition we faced. Not really for their news content, because most were produced on one day a week and not six, but because they were a threat to a paid-for newspaper's advertising.

A free sheet could proudly boast it was carefully delivered to every household in the area but what it couldn't guarantee was that it would be read, cover to cover, by everybody in that household. Generally, if someone took the time and trouble to buy a newspaper, it was a fair indication they intended to read it but you couldn't always say the same for a publication which arrived, unannounced and uninvited, through your letter box.

Then there was the arrival of local radio. With news on the hour, every hour, right through the day, there was no longer any need for people to wait until the Echo hit the streets. News, even local news, was becoming far more instantaneous.

One of our editors could see the threat only too well. On the day that BBC Radio Lincolnshire went on the air for the first time, he allowed a one-line story to appear marking the event. It must have been one of the shortest stories we had ever printed. Later editors, who could see there were ways the two media could work together, were to have a very different attitude.

The arrival of commercial radio was another threat. This time it wasn't just the news stories they were out to capture, it was the Echo's advertising revenue as well.

All the while regional television was improving. Stations were broadcasting round the clock. Teletext and the internet all added to the problems facing newspapers.

I could still remember the days when the Echo's sales hit 40,000 - and that wasn't to be sniffed at in a circulation area where our largest centre of population was under 80,000.

There was a time when I used to joke that taking the Echo regularly was a bit like smoking. It didn't necessarily do you any good but you couldn't give it up. Sadly this didn't seem to be proving the case any more. During times of recession and we seemed to be having more than our fair share of them locally and nationally, people begin to look around to make economies and newspapers seem to be among the first to suffer.

But if we were losing ground on news stories, then we still reigned supreme when it came to the Births, Deaths and Marriages section.

How many times did you overhear one person say to another in a crowded bar or on a busy bus: "Did you see who was dead in the Echo last night?"

I used to have this mental picture of someone opening their copy of the paper and a pile of bones dropping out.

We were very good at features, in-depth investigations and pictures as well. But you had to be a very optimistic type to confidently predict that newspapers, which like the Echo had been set up in the 19th century, would still be around in another one hundred years time.

As we entered 2005, we began to notice some dark

clouds hovering around the horizon. The winds of change were beginning to blow through our newspaper group but I suppose we had all been lulled into a false sense of security by the fact that our own newspaper was still making money. Many of us had thought that no matter what changes could be made in other parts of the building, the editorial section could never be touched because they would always need people to write the stories.

Sadly it wasn't to be the case and in 2005 we noticed one or two people disappearing from our own floor. But, from my own point of view, the year was to be a pretty memorable one. In the early spring, the Derby, Notts, Mid and South Lincs Section of the Showmen's Guild of Great Britain honoured me at their annual civic dinner in Nottingham by presenting me with a Certificate of Appreciation.

The honour was very special to me because it came from people I had always held in the highest regard and I was fortunate enough to receive another honour later in the year.

I first got wind of it when Tony Gadd, who had gone from the category of "Contact" to "Friend" over years of Echo stories, called in at the office one morning. He was clerk to the Gild of Freemen and Lady Freemen of the City of Lincoln (and yes, they really do spell Gild that way!)

Would I be interested in becoming an Honorary Freeman?

Would I? I almost snatched his hand off. Of course I would. Throughout its long history the Gild had only ever conferred the honour on three people - the civic manager, the Mayor's Officer and a former Mayor who dedicated his life to the city. I was quite convinced I didn't deserve the honour, so I quickly said yes before he could chance his mind.

The official letter arrived a week or so later and it was arranged that at the beginning of October, I would be invested. The ceremony took place at the centuries-old Guildhall which spans the High Street. Family and friends were there and it was a very special occasion, particularly when I realised I was the only Lincoln journalist and the only clown to be admitted as an Honorary Freeman of the city.

Don't get the wrong idea by the way. It doesn't mean I have got the Freedom of the City and I can't march down the High Street with a fixed bayonet (or a fixed anything, if it comes to that).

Apparently, if I lived within the city boundaries, I might be eligible to receive the sum of £20 a year, and I might once have been able to graze a sheep or a cow on one or the other of the city commons. But as I haven't got one and I am not planning to get one in the immediate future, I don't think it matters all that much.

But it was a tremendous honour and it's something that I shall never forget.

So that's it. After almost 44 years in newspapers in Lincoln, I have taken what they call "early retirement" or "redundancy" depending on who you are talking to and why. And I must admit I am enjoying every minute of it.

I certainly haven't got to the point of deliberately wandering past the Echo building, gazing longingly up at the editorial floor windows and wishing I was back there inside.

Over the years people always told me: "I have been happily retired for a long time now and I don't know how I ever found the time to do a full-time job."

Perhaps, privately, I used to wonder what on earth

they were talking about but now I have officially joined the ranks of the retired, I know exactly. I thoroughly enjoyed my work, as you can probably gather, and I count myself very lucky and very fortunate to have had a job which I have generally enjoyed doing. At least I have never dreaded the arrival of Monday morning, knowing that it signalled the start of another week of hell.

You may never have realised that what you were doing was particularly very important, until the moment you ask someone if you can have a week's holiday and then you immediately find you have become indispensable.

I have never made a fortune out of working in newspapers but then I haven't starved either and along the way I have met and interviewed the people I would almost certainly never have met in any other occupation.

And if the first chapters of this book have illustrated anything at all, it should be that being a newspaper reporter isn't so much of a job as a way of life.

Send in the Clowns!

Chapter Eight

Humble Beginnings

It was one of those life-defining moments when you find yourself gripped with fear. These days, I suppose they would call it a "panic attack" but in the first few weeks of January 1967, we still referred to it as "being scared stiff" and I think that was a far better description.

The reason for my fear was that I was about to take my first faltering footsteps out onto the stage, as a juggler. True it maybe wasn't the very first time I had ever appeared in a show. My mother would occasionally remind me of the time when I was five years old and I played the King in the school Christmas play.

But this was to be my very first public appearance as a juggler and as I stood in the wings at the North Kesteven Grammar School at North Hykeham, on the edge of Lincoln, I was wondering what on earth had possessed me to volunteer to do it.

There were two very conflicting thoughts running through my mind. One was: "Hurry up and reach the spot in the show when it's time for me to go on and get it over with" and the other was: "Keep the whole thing going as slowly as you can, to put off the fateful moment."

And the section of the stage that I was about to occupy seemed ridiculously small as well. It was no more than two or three paces from the curtain to the edge of the stage.

One moment's lapse in concentration and I would topple straight off the stage and right onto the front row of the audience.

If I dropped anything, then it was almost certain to go bouncing off the stage never to be seen again.

There I stood, quite literally shaking at the knees, awaiting the moment when the scene would come to an end and I would step out onto the stage.

So how had I ever got to this point in my life? I suppose it had started when I was four or five years old, and I was taken to see a circus on Lincoln South Common. It wasn't the biggest circus in the world and it almost certainly wasn't the best but it left a lasting impression on me. From that moment I knew that I wanted to be a part of a travelling circus.

I suppose most children must have wanted that at one time or another. But in those days, when you more or less had to be born into the business to become a circus performer, there didn't seem to be any real possibility of it happening. However it didn't stop me and I suppose my early schooldays were spent encouraging my friends to put on circus performances on street corners.

I have never been particularly good at gymnastics, so acrobatics were out. I once rigged up a very basic trapeze and suspended it from the branch of a tree in our garden. But it didn't take me very long to realise that I was never destined to be a great aerial artiste.

So I suppose, by a process of elimination, I arrived at the point when I decided I would try to be a juggler.

I well remember tossing tennis balls from one hand to another in the school playground, while most of the other boys were kicking a football about or playing cricket, depending on what time of the year it was.

Whenever there was a juggler on television I would always make a point of watching him closely in the hope of picking up a few tips.

But in the late 1950s and early 1960s, it wasn't easy to buy juggling equipment. Most jugglers I saw used indian clubs, which you couldn't seem to buy in shops - at least not the sort of shops which filled Lincoln's main streets. But I eventually solved my problem by finding a sports shop which sold solid wooden medicine clubs to order. They weighed a pound and a half each and it wasn't long before I started to build up some reasonably-strong arm muscles through regular practice.

Because they were plain wood, I decided to brighten them up by painting them gold and I would practice every night standing at the side of my bed. I chose the spot for two reasons. When I dropped a club, as I frequently did, it would land on my bed and I wouldn't have so far to go to retrieve it. And also if it crashed onto the floor, it would produce shouts of protest from my parents and elder sister who were in the room below.

I suppose by the mid-1960s I had got what I had thought was a reasonable juggling act - although, looking back, it couldn't possibly have lasted more than three or four minutes. In addition to the clubs and tennis balls, I had bought myself three plastic plates which I used to spin on the end of sticks and juggle with.

It still wasn't clear in my own mind, just where I was going to show off my newly-acquired skills. When I was rehearsing, I would picture myself standing in front of a large and appreciative audience in a theatre or in a circus Big Top.

But it looked as though my dream was never

going to be fulfilled, until the day I met one of the stalwarts of the North Hykeham Amateur Dramatic Society, Eileen Lingard. I had been assigned to North Hykeham to find as many news stories as possible for the Lincolnshire Chronicle and it meant one or two afternoons a week racing round the town on my Lambretta and calling on some wonderful people who knew everything there was to know about the community.

My newsgathering took me to the school house where Mrs. Lingard lived and between feeding me with generous helpings of her home-made chocolate cake, she would keep me up to date with the latest news on the dramatic society.

In 1967, they were to present their first pantomime. It was quite an ambitious production of Aladdin, and one problem they had was how to cover a scene change. Towards the end of the pantomime the curtains would have to close and the back stage crew needed three or four minutes to get everything ready for the finale.

I don't know how or why I said it - perhaps it was after a particularly generous helping of chocolate cake - but I offered to fill in the gap with my juggling act.

The offer was quickly (perhaps too quickly) accepted and I duly went to my first rehearsal. I was given a small part as well, as a Chinese policeman. And I must admit, I had a whale of a time as the rehearsals went on for week after week.

Then came the day of the show. The moment of truth had arrived and I was standing in the wings waiting for my big entry. Someone murmured "Good luck" into my ear. The curtains began to close and I walked out onto the stage. I wasn't going straight into my routine. I didn't feel confident enough to appear solo on stage, so I was to announce to the audience that I usually appeared with an assistant who couldn't be with me that evening.

That was the cue for Eileen, who by that time was sitting in the audience, to volunteer herself to join me on stage to help out. The idea seemed to work out pretty well and Eileen's presence on stage, was a terrific boost to my confidence. After all she had appeared on the amateur stage so many times, she must have seen and done it all. And her confidence seemed to rub off on me.

There may have been just 50 people watching the show but I felt I had accomplished something, and perhaps it hadn't gone too badly. There were slightly more people in the audience the following night, while for the Saturday matinee the hall was full and there was a three-figure audience for the final performance.

Unless you have ever taken part in an amateur dramatic society production, you can't begin to understand how you feel when it's all over. You get a tremendous feeling of anti-climax. For week after week you have been going to rehearsals, learning lines, trying on costumes and hoping you wouldn't let everybody else down. Then you get three days when you seem to be permanently on a high. And then suddenly it's all over.

You say goodbye to your new-found friends - Aladdin, Widow Twankey, the Emperor, the dancers and the singers. You stop being a Chinese policeman. You stop being the man who juggled with indian clubs, plates and tennis balls and you go back to your everyday job again.

I may well have been scared stiff for most of my few minutes in the spotlight but having enjoyed my first taste of the world of show business I wanted more and soon…

I had to wait just a little more than three months before my next opportunity to appear on stage and once again it was with members of the North Hykeham Amateur Dramatic Society. They were presenting a concert at a primary school in the town to help raise money for a new swimming pool.

I needed a name for the act and I had chosen El Petanos. The "Pet" part came from the first three letters of my Christian name, and the "an" was taken from my partner's Christian name, who was joining me on stage to make sure I had the right props at the right time - and also to give me a bit more confidence.

Looking back I suppose I should have chosen a more simpler name and certainly because there were two of us, I should have gone for "Los" rather than "El" but having made the choice I have stayed with it ever since. It's a name that very few people have ever succeeded in spelling properly, and among the variations I have seen in print over the years have been El Petanus, El Patanos, El Petonas, El Petanas, El Pejanos, El Petanoes, El Patanoes, El Petranos, El Patinos, El Petanof, El Potanos, Los Petanos, El Patarios, El Petano, El Potoras, Los Petinos, El Petannos and my two personal favourites, Elpatanus and E. I. Petanos.

And I am ashamed to say that at least some of those printing errors have been committed by both the Lincoln newspapers I have worked for over the past 44 years.

I remember the name has also caused a succession of comperes and ringmasters a great deal of trouble as well. Many is the time someone would rush up to me at the last minute in the dressing room, before going on stage, and ask: "How exactly do you pronounce your name?"

On one occasion, the compere gave up completely and after the third attempt, simply introduced us as "Old Potatoes!"

By the time I arrived on the stage of the swimming pool concert, I had progressed to a slightly longer spot than before, occupying the best part of two records, so I guess that meant I was on stage for something like five or six minutes.

To extend the act, I had managed to work out some new tricks including one where my partner would kneel down on stage, holding a drum, which I would somehow manage to beat with the clubs as I juggled with them. I also added four large rings, which I painted silver and a very ancient tennis racket which I think had been my mother's in her younger days.

There was a full house of something like 150 people and the new act was well and truly born.

But it was a good job I didn't rely on my juggling skills - such as they were - as a major source of income, because bookings were few and far between and I was still a long way off having the courage to charge for my services.

The summer came and went and we were well into the autumn by the time of my next show, which was once again at the North Kesteven Grammar School in North Hykeham, for another charity concert by the amateur dramatic society. My routine hadn't changed a great deal since April, except now I was juggling with three tennis rackets.

I had finally pensioned off my mother's ancient racket and bought three from one of the High Street chain stores in Lincoln for, I think, something like a pound or so each - so it represented something of a big cash investment for me.

It perhaps says something for the quality of the tennis rackets that 39 years and something like 1,400 shows later, I was still using them.

Christmas brought us a handful of bookings in Lincoln. At last we had arrived in "the big city", but again they were charity events. Although they may not have done a lot for my career or for juggling in general, I remember feeling particularly pleased the day I spotted the city Mayor among the audience.

For the next couple of years, I found I was having to concentrate more on my work as a journalist and a lot of big things were happening in my life, including the birth of my first daughter, Karen-Louise. But I was still doing pantomimes and something called "A Sausage and Chip Supper" with the North Hykeham amateurs.

At around that time I was to meet a family who - although they may never have known it - were to play a major part in my future career. They were the Yelding family, Andy and Dolly and their son Bobby. Some years previously they had appeared in some of the biggest circuses in the country. Dolly did a ballerina on horseback routine and walked a tight wire. Andy was a clown and I think possibly a very good acrobat during his younger days and Bobby was a talented all-rounder, clowning, presenting the ponies and rope-spinning, among many other things. He was probably the most talented rope-spinner I have ever come across but such a modest sort of person that you would never have known it in conversation.

By the time I met the family they had their own small circus which was based in Staffordshire during the winter and every summer it used to venture into

Lincolnshire to appear on the village playing fields and the farmers' meadows in the villages, which would otherwise have never seen a circus from one generation to the next.

You would find them in the most unlikely setting in a place you had never heard of but no matter where they were or how well or how badly they were doing, you would always be made most welcome.

I first met the family through either my work at the Lincolnshire Echo or as a correspondent for World's Fair, the showmen's newspaper and we seemed to get on well straight away. I learned so much from watching the performances and I have got to admit some of the tried and tested comedy routines they were doing in the 1970s, I have adapted and I am still doing today in my children's shows.

One night, when the circus was appearing at a village just south of Lincoln, I went over to see the show and because the circus was staying for a second day, there wasn't the usual rush to get the Big Top down after the final performance. So we sat around in the tent watching the night fall and Bobby gave me my first lesson in rope-spinning.

Later that night I went back home, took down the washing line from the backyard and started my own version of what he had shown me. I know I will never ever be as good as Bobby but his tips on rope-spinning led to the start of my second routine.

For a long time I had been thinking about doing a second spot. The juggling act had reached about six minutes which I judged was probably long enough, bearing in mind I was never going to be an international artiste. And, with Bobby's help and encouragement, the rope-spinning became my second act.

I used it in public for the first time at a talent contest at Butlin's Holiday Camp in Skegness during the early summer of 1970. To the accompaniment of the camp's resident organist, I started off my little spot with some very basic rope-spinning and then went on to a slightly shorter version of my juggling routine.

I remember I was petrified by the size of the audience. The old Gaiety Theatre - it has now long been demolished - was a vast building and the talent contest involved two performances, just an hour-and-a-quarter apart and at the second show there were 1,000 people in the auditorium. To someone who had only ever been used to standing in the wings and literally counting the number of people in the audience before I went on, it was a tremendous thing for me to do - and I was probably more scared than I had ever been before.

Luckily, although the weekly talent contests were abundantly blessed with singers, musicians and comedians, they very seldom seemed to include any jugglers. So when it came to the auditions, if the producer wanted to have any sort of balanced programme for his audience, a juggler was almost always bound to get into the show, I reasoned.

Just a few weeks after the talent contest - which, of course, I didn't win - I had my first opportunity to appear with Yelding's Circus. And, funnily enough, it was in the village which, a few years later, was to become my home.

The site was a farmer's field on a corner as you approached the village and it was a lovely July evening.

I remember slipping out of the tent, and looking at the queue waiting to buy tickets at the little booth close to the entrance. I counted around 70 people and, although it wouldn't have filled more than the odd row of seats at many of the bigger shows around at the time, it represented almost a full house for the Yeldings.

My own contribution was the brief juggling act. There was no question of my ever doing rope-spinning in a show where Bobby was appearing, as my act wouldn't have stood any sort of comparison.

By now my costume was a pair of black trousers, with a row of silver braiding stitched down the outside of each leg; a white shirt with a red cummerbund, and a black bow tie.

Thanks to the Yelding family, I had at last achieved my childhood ambition. By July 1970 I was appearing in a real circus. I still wasn't earning any money of course but I think I would quite happily have paid them for the privilege.

We appeared in another village, just south of Scunthorpe, a few weeks later and not long afterwards I had arranged for the circus to appear at Caenby Corner Steam Spectacular. In those days I was among the founder organisers and was the hard-working and unpaid publicity officer for the event.

The rally was masterminded by the now late George Taylor, who was really the driving force behind the small committee and I had managed to convince him that the circus would be a big attraction at the rally, which was held to raise money for Lincolnshire Spastics Centre at Scunthorpe.

When I arrived at the circus tent on the Saturday afternoon I found the Yeldings in a state of panic. It seemed a magpie had perched on the top of the King Pole and they hadn't been able to encourage it to fly away at once. This was apparently a sign of very bad luck.

We did three performances, to very meagre

audiences, throughout the afternoon and it was obvious that Andy, Dolly and Bobby still had the magpie on their minds.

That night, after I had left the field, a terrific gale got up. Some small stalls on the showground were sent spinning and the circus tent was blown down and badly ripped. So maybe there was something in the superstition after all.

The next day with the circus tent out of action, I did a quick look around the ground and spotted a much smaller tent, which the committee had hired for a charity to use.

The charity workers didn't seem to be returning for the second day, so rather than have their tent standing empty, Bobby, Andy and I dismantled it and took it over to where the circus should have been standing. We built it up and managed to get some sort of show on for the afternoon, but when members of the charity turned up and started looking for their tent, I somehow couldn't muster up the courage to tell them what had happened to it.

It was while I was juggling outside the entrance to the tent, trying to encourage people to buy a ticket for the next performance, that a family came up to me and started talking. They had seen the circus in their village a few days earlier and it was obviously still very fresh in their minds.

"Our little girl watched the Moscow State Circus on television the other evening," they began. I immediately started to have a few misgivings. I had seen the programme as well and it was studded with top Russian stars. It was, and still is, one of the world's finest circuses. And Mum and Dad went on: "She watched it right through to the end and then she turned to us and said, 'It was very good but it wasn't as good as OUR circus'."

I must admit I had a lump in my throat. I remembered the evening the family had visited the circus and the little girl had taken part in one of Bobby's routines and ever since then, in her own mind, it had become her circus.

I had learned another, very important lesson from my time with the Yelding family.

If you involve the audience, as they did, the whole thing becomes so much more important to the children and they never forget it.

Chapter Nine

Circus Days

After the circus moved out of Lincolnshire, it was time to take a vacation and we went to a holiday camp in Morecambe where we managed to gain third place in the weekly talent contest, appearing in front of what was the biggest audience so far - something like 2,000 people. I can't remember too much about it now but I bet I was petrified and probably spent most of the previous few hours wondering why on earth I went on putting myself through that kind of ordeal.

In the run-up to Christmas, I turned the rope-spinning into a self-contained little act of its own and briefly donned jeans, checked shirt and a cowboy hat, to become The Wild Westerners but it wasn't a name that was to survive beyond the end of the year.

A few days into 1971 I at long last succeeded in earning some money from the juggling act. I appeared at an Over 60s party in a large village, between Lincoln and Sleaford, and received the magnificent sum of ten shillings (50p) for my trouble.

Nationally times and fashions were changing in the early 1970s and as far as costumes were concerned it was becoming increasingly difficult to keep one step ahead of the audience.

They were sometimes wearing more colourful and sparkling clothes than I was. It was time to say goodbye to the white shirt, the black bow tie and the black trousers, and hello to a pair of red crushed velvet trousers and a tie top which showed a daring glimpse of bare middle. The new costume was worn for the first time when we returned to the Morecambe holiday camp that summer but although we again took part in the weekly talent contest, my new look evidently wasn't enough to impress the judges and we came away without a prize.

The summer again found Yelding's Circus back in Lincolnshire and we went to some wonderful little places with them. There was one very tiny farm field in Wragby, between Lincoln and Horncastle, where the field was so small Bobby had to take down part of the tent every time the farmer needed to drive his tractor out onto the main road.

Business in some places was better than others and I remember once on a playing field on the edge of a village, we worked to just 18 people. But the show went on and it was a tribute to the family that they always put exactly the same effort into every show, no matter how few people there were in the audience.

I suppose the day you do decide to leave things out and cut corners is the day you find that one of the few people in the audience is a television producer or an agent looking for a circus act.

Towards the end of July the circus was among the attractions at a traction engine rally in Louth and it was here that I learned another valuable lesson. The day had started out in glorious sunshine and the crowds were out enjoying the music of the fairground organs and watching a collection of veteran traction engines being put through their paces in the arena.

As usual I had hung my clothes in a hook at the back of the tent after I changed into my costume. During the afternoon the black clouds rolled in, there were claps of thunder and a heavy downpour which sent people scampering into the tent and ensured us of at least one good house. It wasn't until the end of the day, when I went back to collect my clothes, that I found the rain had poured down the walling and they were soaked through. I learned never to leave them there again, no matter how good the weather was at the start of the day.

Although I liked the small villages in the heart of rural Lincolnshire, I liked it best of all when the circus was on the coast. Sometimes between shows, you would take a stroll up to the promenade and try to capture a bit of the holiday spirit, before hurrying back to the circus for the evening performance.

The weather was always very important when the circus was by the sea. If it was hot and sunny, the holidaymakers didn't want to know. They wanted to be enjoying themselves on the beach and in the sea. If it was raining, then they wouldn't come out of their caravans and boarding houses and you could never get them out of the holiday camps anyway, because there was always plenty of free entertainment going on inside.

The best conditions were when it had been raining all day and perhaps an hour before show time, it would fine up and the families were so glad to get out they would come up to the circus just for something to do.

We had one of those days at Chapel St. Leonards, between Mablethorpe and Skegness, when the afternoon show was fuller than I had ever seen it before or since. There were people everywhere. All the benches were filled. Some extra chairs had been found from somewhere. Children were sitting on the grass right up to the ring fence and they were even sitting in front of the entrance to the ring, so you had to clear a way through before you could get in to work.

But the atmosphere was amazing and I was delighted that my Mum and Dad had chosen that particular day to come over and see the show.

As the summer drew to a close it was time for a family holiday and this time we went to Butlin's camp at Pwllheli on the north west coast of Wales. As usual, along with our holiday clothes, we had packed the juggling and rope-spinning props with the weekly talent contest in mind. The audition was held in front of an audience of 800 people at the Gaiety theatre. (I think every theatre at every Butlin camp was called the Gaiety at that time).

I had more reason than usual to be nervous because one of the judges was a professional juggler. We were the last act on, so I had plenty of time to think about it and to get more nervous. But I think the judges must have taken pity on us, because they placed us into the contest which took place over two performances a couple of evenings later. Two acts went through to the camp final at the end of the season and we were one of them.

I couldn't believe it. At last we had won something. Because the end of the season was fast approaching, we had to return to Pwllheli just a couple of weeks later for the finals before the camp closed for the winter. How I managed to get the time off from work, I can't imagine, because with a staff our size it was never easy to get one holiday, let alone to get two holidays within a month.

The camp final was divided into two heats with ten acts going through out of forty from each heat. Again, I think the gods were smiling on us - perhaps through gritted teeth - because we were placed in the camp final the following night. In theory, we were just one show away from the grand final at the

London Palladium but we weren't to get any further.

The Gaiety Theatre was packed for the camp final and I was told there were 2,400 people in the audience. I wouldn't have known because there comes a point when it doesn't matter. It's just sufficient to know there are rows and rows of faces disappearing into the far distance. Again I must have been absolutely terrified.

And if you want to get some idea of the calibre of artistes who you would find in a Butlin talent show in those days, I can tell you the other finalists included unknowns who later went on to become top comedians Cannon and Ball, Les Dennis and Mike Lancaster. And none of us were judged good enough for the grand final. Still, it didn't seem to do the others very much harm, as I once had the pleasure of pointing out to Les Dennis, when I interviewed him many years later, on the day he was appearing at a Lincoln area night spot and I was leisure editor at the Lincolnshire Echo.

My next paid engagement came in January 1972, when I was able to command a fee of £2 to appear at a cricket club dinner and dance in a village just outside Lincoln.

There have been so many changes over the years, that it now seems difficult to think that there was once a time when I used to smoke a cigarette on stage. To provide a bit of light relief, while I was juggling with my indian clubs, my assistant would put a cigarette between my lips and light it, and I would take a few puffs while juggling.

I somehow don't think it would go down too well nowadays and we didn't keep it in the act for very long. The idea came from an agent who thought it would add a touch of humour but I couldn't really see the point.

I was never a very keen smoker anyway. I would occasionally puff on a filter tip for the sake of being sociable in a crowd and then I stopped being sociable and gave up.

Although I didn't know it at the time, 1972 was to turn out to be one of the most important years in my juggling "career". I received the princely sum of £5 to appear on a school stage at a gala queen contest in a village near Sleaford, and had some success in talent contests at Lincoln and Pwllheli. I also took part in a talent show at the Dovercourt Bay holiday camp which was later to find fame as Maplin's in the hit TV comedy series Hi-de-Hi.

And I had the distinction of being possibly the first juggler in living memory ever to appear inside the great nave of Lincoln Cathedral.

It was the cathedral's 900th birthday and all sorts of things were going on, including something called "The Wonder Show" which was being staged inside the ancient building for five nights. They erected something not unlike a boxing or wrestling ring at the west end of the nave and although it was mid-August I remember it was bitterly cold, especially when the massive doors were opened and the evening breeze used to whip inside.

I changed inside a small tent alongside the ring and I had the tomb of, I think, a former Bishop, for company. It seemed strange to be stripping off night after night inside the cathedral, as hundreds of visitors walked past the tent without noticing.

It was also the last summer I was to spend with the Yeldings. By now Andy had died and Bobby and his mother were doing their best to carry on but Dolly was having problems with her eyesight and things must have been so very difficult for them both. It was a credit to them that they were still able to put on an entertaining show.

One of my most abiding memories of their shows was seeing Dolly perform her tight wire routine to the music "Hello Dolly". Even now, years after her death, whenever I hear that tune played, my mind always goes back to those very special days with the Yelding family.

It was while I was appearing with them one Sunday towards the end of August that I met a man who was to play a major part in my life. James Brothers Circus was nearing the end of its annual summer season at Mablethorpe and was shortly moving inland to start the autumn leg of its tour. The owner, Jimmy Fossett, came over to see the Yeldings - they must have been old friends - and he saw my juggling act.

Jimmy had got one or two larger towns than usual to play in Lincolnshire during the coming weeks, and wondered if I would be interested in doing my juggling act in his show for a few days.

I didn't really need to think twice before saying yes. Yelding's Circus was about to move out of the area, and James Brothers Circus and Zoo was a larger outfit. It was a chance which was too good to miss, and yet I had a few niggling doubts. Would I be good enough for the bigger show?

I offered to do a try-out first in Horncastle, where the show was to spend a couple of days before going on to Scunthorpe and Lincoln. After a day's work at the office, I arrived in time for the night show and found 350 people in the audience. But it wasn't them I was so worried about. Many of the circus people were curious about this juggling journalist who had appeared from nowhere, and everyone, who wasn't doing anything more important, was standing around the tent to see me work.

It was a bit of an unnerving experience but things couldn't have gone too badly because it was to be the start of a long and very happy association with Jim and his circus.

In those days I didn't work on a Monday at the Echo. My working week ran from Tuesday to Saturday, so it meant I was free to go to Scunthorpe to take part in both shows on the opening night. The ground in those days was the Manley Street Playing Field alongside the railway line and almost in the shadow of one of the town's famous steelworks. Also making his first appearance with the circus that day was a young local lad called Bill Tate, who clowned under the name of Bilbo, and went on to work very successfully in the circus profession for a long time.

From Scunthorpe the circus moved to a one-off site right in the middle of Lincoln. The ground had started out as railway sidings alongside St. Mark's station but by the early 1970s, the tracks had been taken up, and the area had been turned into a car park to serve a nearby supermarket. The circus was there for a week, and although the first show was at five o'clock, I could generally get down in time for the start because I finished work around half past four.

I remember one day during the week, when I was held up reporting an inquest at the County Hospital. I raced my Lambretta - as fast as you can race anything through the teatime traffic in Lincoln - and got to the circus to hear the music playing for the performing pigs.

Yes really. Jim had a couple of very large Warwickshire pigs which used to do a creditable routine jumping hurdles and opening gates and at this time, my juggling act used to go on next. I couldn't help thinking that there was some significance in this.

Despite my late arrival, I still managed to get changed and ready in time to go on as usual. Apart from my juggling act I also used to take part in the finale as a red indian. My contribution to it was to squat on one side of the ring and beat a tom-tom drum while other red indians in the centre of the ring, worked with a number of very large snakes.

Of all the circus creatures I have ever shared the sawdust ring with, I think snakes are my least favourite and although I have very occasionally been known to touch or stroke one, that's as far as it has ever gone. Nothing would induce me to have one wrapped around my shoulders, so I used to keep a very wary eye on the snakes while I was around the circus.

The next venue for the circus was just a little bit different. When Jim told me the circus was pulling down after the Saturday night in Lincoln to travel around 18 miles to the little village of Dorrington for a one-off show on the following afternoon, it didn't seem to make sense. The circus, with its two-mast Big Top, and capable of seating close on 1,000 people, usually went to the larger towns and cities.

But there was a special significance about Dorrington. It seemed that five years into the 20th century a travelling circus had just arrived in the village when disaster had struck. A one-year-old called Harry Fossett, upset a cauldron of boiling water over himself and was scalded to death. He was buried in the village churchyard, and was the only member of the prominent circus family to be buried outside the family graves in Warwickshire.

Eventually the circus had carried on its way but

the villagers always tended the grave carefully and as far as I know they still do to this day. And because of the villagers' kindness, Jim had decided to take the whole circus to a farmer's field down Dorrington Fen to give a charity show to raise money for the church to say thank you.

What a day it was. The show was due to start at four o'clock and long before then it was packed. Something like 200 people had to be turned away because there wasn't any room for them and the number inside the Big Top must have exceeded the entire population of the village.

I well remember the Vicar, the Reverend Arthur Beverley, who gave an address in the ring, telling the audience: "The circus people and I are the only ones working in Dorrington today."

It was while I was appearing with the circus just a couple of weeks later at Melton Mowbray that Jim asked if I would like to travel with the show instead of commuting once a week as and when I was able to get over. And I must admit I thought long and hard before reluctantly saying no.

It was everything I had ever wanted to do. Apart from doing a spot or two in the ring, I would also act as something like front of house manager, and drive a fairly sizeable van pulling a trailer behind. The money was just about good enough to be able to keep the mortgage on for my home in Lincoln, but there was no guarantee that my job at the Echo would still have been there at the end of the season.

In the end I let my head rule my heart and made the decision not to go and to be absolutely honest I am sure that, with hindsight, it was the best thing to do.

Around about this time I was appearing fairly

regularly in the cabaret room of a large new pub on the edge of a Lincoln estate. It didn't pay a great deal but it was all experience. Admission to the room was generally free but on one memorable occasion, when comedian the now late Colin Crompton was topping the bill, I think a charge of £1 was made.

The two most memorable things about the stage, from my point of view, was that it seemed incredibly narrow, especially bearing in mind I shared it with an organist and drummer and there were large mirrors on the wall facing the stage. The temptation was to look at yourself in the mirror while you were working, but if you did that your concentration went straight away and it played havoc with the juggling act.

What many people watching a cabaret, especially in a pub or private members' club, may not realise is that the dressing room backstage probably leaves a lot to be desired.

If you have thoughts about artistes lounging around in comfortable armchairs, sipping drinks before making up in front of a mirror surrounded by a dozen light bulbs, then you should think again.

Some are it's true but a lot aren't and over the years I have changed in anything from a large cupboard to a board room and from the back of a lorry to a hotel kitchen.

One tiny club, in what the estate agents would describe as "a very sought-after village" just outside Lincoln at the start of 1973, didn't have anywhere at all where an artiste could change and when I did a children's party there, I had no alternative but to stand outside the back door and change. And you had to bear in mind this was still the middle of January.

There was no way I was ever going to become

part of a globe-trotting cabaret or circus act but that doesn't mean to say I have never had the pleasure of appearing outside the British Isles. The first time happened during the early summer of 1973.

Lincoln has a very long and very successful twinning link with the wine-growing city of Neustadt in what used to be called West Germany. I am not quite sure which member of the city council had the idea of twinning with Neustadt but whoever it was would be assured of my vote for life. Because as cities go Neustadt is one of the nicest I have ever visited and the people are terrific, very friendly and perhaps best of all, they speak fluent English.

Having heard so many good things about it, I decided I would like to take the family for a trip to Neustadt and I thought it would be nice if I could perhaps spread a bit of goodwill while I was there. Bands, choirs, sports groups and dancers had all gone over there but as far as I knew Lincoln had never sent a juggler before.

I contacted Robin Rushton, who was the city council's expert on tourism and explained what I wanted to do. He got in touch with his opposite number in Neustadt and I was assured we would be able to do some free shows in schools and hospitals while we were there. So I loaded as many of my props as possible into the boot of my ancient Vauxhall Viva and we set off - at a steady 40 mph - bound for Neustadt.

Among all the other problems I had to overcome before setting off for foreign parts, was one which I bet doesn't trouble many a British tourist bound for Germany. I don't know whether or not it still applies but in the early 1970s at least there was what seemed to be a very unusual restriction on foreign travellers.

113

No adult was permitted to take more than one tennis racket into the country. Why, I do not know but what I did know was I had three of them among my props and I needed them as the finale to my juggling act.

Happily my car wasn't searched at the border. If it had been, my abundance of tennis rackets could have taken just a bit of explaining away.

Now, as anyone who has ever travelled with me for any length of time will tell you, I am not famous for being the world's fastest driver - especially on roads in countries which are unfamiliar to me. So it took us several days before we arrived in Germany and duly reported to the man in the town hall.

That was where we got a bit of a shock, because the Germans - as we quickly found out - are expert when it comes to organising things. I was presented with an itinery which contained a list of twenty-one shows we were to give at twenty venues in just four days. And because I didn't know the area at all, someone was being provided to drive in front of our car and once we arrived at the venues, she would look after our young daughter, Karen, while the show went on.

It was obvious straight away, that we were going to be operating to a very tight time schedule and we had to trim the shows to something like twenty minutes each to fit them in. There would be no time for costume changes, so once the costumes went on for the first show, they wouldn't come off again until we were back in the hotel at the end of the day.

We arrived at the first school to start at nine o'clock, and we quickly realised we were having the senior schools in the morning, and the kindergartens in the afternoons. I just couldn't believe the reception we had at the first school. There were something like

114

500 students in the hall, and at the end of our little show, we were quite literally mobbed. It was pretty much like the sort of reception The Beatles used to get in their hey day and in our case it was completely unjustified. No false modesty here. Trust me, it was completely unjustified.

We autographed everything that was pushed under our noses, while trying desperately to get the props back into the car for the journey to the next school and trying to ensure the lady from the town hall was keeping an eye on our little daughter.

"Surely that was just a one-off, it won't happen again," we reasoned as we sped through the outskirts of the city on the way to the next school. But it wasn't. To this day, I have never understood why we got such a reception at the senior schools in Neustadt. The kindergartens tended to be a lot easier to handle, and there were fewer children as well. But by the end of the first day, when we had done six twenty-minute shows, in just a little over six hours, we felt shattered.

We had the weekend to enjoy the council's freedom of the lovely open-air swimming pool, in the warm May sunshine, with the vine-covered hillsides rising up all around. Then on the Monday morning, with even the lady from the town hall looking just a little bit worried about what we had taken on, we launched into another five schools between 9am and 3p.m. and we rounded off the day at what I think was probably the local library, where we did two more performances.

And so it went on. I vaguely remember we were over-running by so much, we missed out a school somewhere, although we did manage to pull it in before the end of the holiday. One of the city's bergermeisters did us the honour of attending our final performance, introducing us to the students, before taking us out for a farewell lunch.

It had been a tremendous experience and perhaps the reason why I have never tried to do it again is because nothing could ever compare with the reception we got on that occasion.

Later in the summer we spent an enjoyable few days holiday with James Brothers Circus. Every summer, the show would go to the little family resort of Mablethorpe, and stay from the beginning of July until early September.

It seldom did bumper business there, although it did follow a pattern. Saturdays were usually quiet, as families were just arriving and looking around to see what the place had to offer. Most circuses didn't open on Sundays in those days, so the busiest time came from Monday to Wednesday - depending on the weather. By Thursday money was getting tight and by Friday people were packing to go home.

The big advantage from the circus's point of view was that it meant they didn't have to travel for a few weeks and there were savings with publicity, because once the posters had been put up many of them wouldn't come down again until the end of the run.

For once I was able to feel like a real circus performer, retiring to the luxury of a small touring caravan which Jim had kindly provided for us while we were with him.

For the next season Jim had engaged a juggler to travel with the show full time, so I wasn't spending most of my days off travelling to and from the show.

So I decided this was the time to try something just a little bit different. Instead of waiting for people to book my acts for parties and galas, I teamed up with an old friend called Dennis Black, who lived in

Lincoln and like me he was a huge circus fan. When he wasn't busy with his full-time job as chief projectionist at the local ABC cinema, he was better known to countless children in and around Lincoln, as Bimbo the Clown.

His speciality was magic and together we were able to put on a respectably-long show, aimed primarily at the children. We hired a number of village halls around Lincolnshire. We had good quality posters printed, which we pinned to notice boards in the area and badgered the village shops into displaying some in their windows.

This was what they call "billing" in the circus world and it was a job I have always hated. If the first shopkeeper of the day said no, or was even reluctant to display a poster, then that was my courage gone for the rest of the day. I would even feel guilty about displaying one on the notice board outside the village hall itself.

With Bimbo's wife, Betty, taking the tickets at the door and selling orange juice and sweets at the interval, we tried to create something of a circus atmosphere and we kept to the villages which we knew hadn't seen a proper circus for years.

The show would generally start at 6.30p.m., and on the very first night, I remember opening the door at six o'clock, and looking hopefully up the street to catch sight of the first youngster heading our way. But the street was deserted.

Fortunately for us, by the time the curtain went up, there were around 50 in the audience and we had a satisfactory show. But when we reckoned up the takings afterwards, the total profit from the venture was less than £10, which didn't seem to be a fair return for all our efforts, especially by the time we had divided the cash between us.

We carried on with the venture at various times throughout the summer and to within a few weeks of Christmas. Nowhere was ever a complete disaster but although we made money, the profit was never more than a pound or two each. And while we were no doubt having fun, we could only really afford to carry on doing it at times when there were no better paid jobs coming in.

Chapter Ten

The Trials and Tribulations of a Juggler

As 1975 dawned, I was feeling a little more confident with every show we did. There was still the fear of the unknown, like wondering how big the stage would be. Would the audience be within touching distance? Would the lighting be shining straight into my eyes making it difficult to see what I was doing? Even, how low would the ceiling be.

If you are a comedian or a singer, problems like that can't figure very highly in your list of things to worry about. But if you happen to be a juggler, who has to move around quite a lot and throw objects into the air with the idea of catching them again, then you do tend to need quite a bit of space.

I remember once arriving at a club before the audience came in, standing on the stage and placing my hands flat against the ceiling. There was no way I could have done the complete routine with such a low headroom and I ended up doing most of the act on the floor immediately in front of the curtains.

That summer was the final time I ever went in for a talent contest - not because I felt I was above that sort of thing but because I was beginning to feel they weren't worth all the pressure. So after a final appearance in the Butlin Star Trail National Talent Contest at Ayr, sadly the only occasion I have ever appeared in Scotland, I did a Pub Entertainer of the Year contest at a Lincoln pub and bowed gracefully out of the competition scene.

There used to be a very nice hotel not far from the centre of Lincoln. It must have started out as a private house and it was gradually extended to become The Annesley. Although it was never going to be the biggest hotel in the city, it did boast something that none of the others had. There was a compact little cabaret room and it attracted some of the biggest names in the country.

How they were able to do it, I have no idea, because the capacity was very tiny but they booked people like Harry Secombe, Frankie Vaughan, Arthur Askey and Frank Ifield, and they never charged a lot of money for a ticket either. When you went, it was a bit like watching some of the biggest names in show business appearing in your own front room.

I appeared there for three consecutive nights in October in a cabaret put on by a local amateur operatic and dramatic society, who must have recently finished, or were about to do, the musical Oklahoma. Because I remember having to sing the title song in the finale along with the rest of the company.

What made those shows so very special for me was that the music for my juggling act was provided by Arthur Mayall, who had been one of my teachers at Junior and later at Secondary Modern School in Lincoln. He was a very talented musician and when he wasn't busy teaching, he had his own trio of musicians appearing at clubs in and around the city.

Until around this time I always had a bit of a fear (combined perhaps with hatred) of actually standing up on a stage and talking to an audience for any length of time. As a juggler and rope-spinner there weren't naturally many opportunities to engage the audience in a lengthy conversation. But all that was to change the evening I was appearing at a club in Lincoln.

The man in charge of the disco had agreed to play the records for me at the right time or so I thought. I had just gone through the process of introducing myself to the audience and had uttered those fateful words: "I would now like to start off with my rope-spinning." But when I turned round to cue the man in charge of the records, he wasn't anywhere to be seen.

I did a bit of a double take and I think the audience must have thought it was all part of the show but I was getting increasingly worried by the second. Eventually, someone realised the disco man must have wondered off into the bar in the next room, so someone was hurridly despatched to retrieve him. Meanwhile I was left with a microphone in my hand and I had to stand and talk to the audience until the man re-appeared.

To this day I can't remember what I said but by the end of it all a very short spot had been turned into quite a long one and I had overcome one of my greatest fears - the hard way.

It all stood me in good stead for the following summer when I was booked for seven Tuesday evenings at Trusville Holiday Estate in Mablethorpe. I can't quite remember how I came to get the booking but it was to be a very important one and it gave me a chance to work with the camp's resident entertainments manager, the now late Ken Turner and the resident children's entertainer, Paul Kane.

Paul was always a great chap to work with, and the idea was my partner and I would do two twenty-minute spots with the juggling and rope-spinning acts augmented by some tried and tested circus comedy routines, like "You can't play here" and a competition where the children had to make hats out of sheets of newspaper.

All fairly basic stuff but the children seemed to love it. We even had our own ghost, with my partner in a skeleton mask and a white sheet draped around her.

I have always loved working to holiday camp audiences and sometimes we had as many as six hundred children in the dance hall, while their parents enjoyed themselves in the licensed club a few hundred yards away.

But much as I loved the place, I don't think I would have swapped places with Paul as the resident entertainer. We only had to cope with the children for less than an hour once a fortnight. He had to keep them amused during just about every waking hour for six days a week right through the season. Whatever he was paid, I am sure it was nowhere near enough.

When I first heard that 1977 was to be celebrated as the Queen's Silver Jubilee, it didn't take me long to realise it could be quite a good year for us as well. It seemed as if just about every street in Lincoln, every village in the county, was going to have its own party or gala to mark the occasion.

It had the potential of being another Christmas but most of the activities were being concentrated over just the one weekend in early June. Everybody wanted entertainment but rather than rushing madly from one venue to another, we decided to limit ourselves to just one a day.

We appeared at a school in Horncastle on the day the town's inner relief road (appropriately enough named Jubilee Way) was opened and some village halls but heavy rain washed out an open-air party we were to have done on the Jubilee day itself. By coincidence history was to repeat itself twenty-five years later, when heavy rain once again washed out an outdoor show we were to have done in a mining village near Doncaster on Golden Jubilee Day.

The holiday weekend coincided with the start of our second season at Trusville. This time we were there for nine weeks and because many of the holidaymakers returned year after year, we couldn't go back with exactly the same show, so I brought in one or two new comedy routines and daughter Karen joined us in the finale, which involved waving lengthy strips of ribbon around to music.

There wasn't a lot of skill to what we called our Disco Ribbon Finale but it looked reasonably spectacular and it was a good way of finishing off the show. The only snag was you couldn't do it on moderately-sized stages because the ribbons would get tangled up and the whole thing could end in disaster. And also if the audience was too close, you ran he risk of flicking the end of the ribbons into someone's face.

Now, I have never been a great expert when it comes to Do-It-Yourself. I have almost reached the stage of having to call in an electrician every time a fuse goes and I have to screw up quite a bit of courage just to change a light bulb.

So it must have come as a big surprise to those who knew me, when they discovered I was making many of my own props for the show.

There were three which I was particularly proud of and they were all constructed from the very basic household materials. The presenters of Blue Peter would have been so proud.

The first was something I called "The Rock Factory". You must have seen the conjuror or the clown try to bake a cake and, although he puts in all the correct ingredients, everything goes wrong at the last minute and he ends up with a dead chicken or something. Well, I worked out my own version of this where I tried to make "genuine seaside rock" using a rock-making machine, which I had discovered someone had given me as a surprise present.

The machine was basically a cardboard box from a Lincoln supermarket - the sort they used to have near to the checkouts so you could put your shopping in them to carry home. You don't seem to see that nowadays. It's all plastic bags or "bags for life".

This cardboard box I provided with a secret compartment so young volunteers from the audience could put the ingredients in, and when they opened the little door at the bottom, they would get their "genuine seaside rock". But of course, instead of the sticky teeth-smashing kind which we all love, it was a chunk of rock I had picked up from the nearby beach.

The beach also provided one of the other vital ingredients for it all. The sand doubled as sugar. Simple but effective humour and it's good for at least five minutes. Almost thirty years on, I am still using the same routine - and the same cardboard box. They were built to last in those days.

My second "gadget" was just a little bit more adventurous and although I don't use it in the show these days, I haven't ruled out the fact that it may one day return.

I had long been a fan of the clowns' exploding cars in the circus and I saw how much the children love them. So I thought I would have my own version. It wasn't practical to have a car, so I came up with the household tool that just about every child would recognise straight away - a vacuum cleaner.

The idea was my partner would be trying to read a piece of serious poetry to the audience but she would be interrupted by my efforts to clean up. I bought a cylinder vacuum cleaner for £1 and took out all the mechanical parts. I then substituted a front door buzzer, a machine that blew bubbles out the end, a cycle hooter, a pair of knickers on the end of a short length of washing line, a spring snake which jumped out of a little opening and a child's potty.

It all combined to produce a routine which could run for anything up to seven minutes, depending on the reaction of the audience.

The third prop, which I was particularly proud of, was an old pedal bin which I converted into a washing machine, by adding a number of dials and the inevitable front door buzzer. The idea was that I would attempt to wash a very important handkerchief but of course by changing the item over inside the "machine", it would come out in turn as very small, very large, in tatters or with a big hole in the middle of it.

All simple stuff but it was fairly easy to construct and best of all - with the exception of the bubble machine in the vacuum cleaner - it was all pretty cheap as well.

After the fun of taking our own little show round the village halls, I had wanted to give the idea another try and this time Paul Kane, with his magic routines, provided the ideal partner. When the Mablethorpe season finished, we tried a number of village halls around Lincolnshire, performing this time on Sunday afternoons.

Again we had some good quality posters printed. We had some flyers done and took a lot of time and trouble to ensure that people in the villages knew the show was coming. There was one occasion when I personally put leaflets through the letterboxes of every house on the village's largest council estate. But, if anything, numbers in the audience were smaller than before and we never made anything more than a pound or two from every performance.

When Bimbo first asked if we would like to do a show with him in London, I must admit I was just a little bit worried. I had tended to concentrate on the smaller towns and villages, where they probably never saw a juggler from one year to the next and couldn't easily compare me with the better ones.

But the people in London could see the lot, and they didn't necessarily have to go to the top-priced clubs and theatres to do it. There were jugglers, far better than I could ever hope to be, busking in the streets almost every day. Then there was the prospect of driving to and from London in the day and finding my way around the place when I got there.

But Bimbo's suggestion was such a tempting one that I couldn't really say no. He was a member of Clowns International - it's a brotherhood which many clowns belong to and Bimbo was a long-standing member.

Every year at the beginning of February they held a memorial service in the clowns' church of Holy Trinity in Dalston, for Joey Grimaldi, who is regarded by many as one of the greatest clowns who ever lived and an inspiration to generations of others.

Because of him, clowns all over the world are often known as "Joeys".

The idea was we would all attend the church service in costume and afterwards the clowns put on a show in the adjoining church hall for something like five hundred children. Bimbo had the chance of taking part in the show and he wanted us to provide the only non-clown act in the programme.

But when we got there, we found it wasn't just children in the audience. There was a sprinkling of circus personalities as well and when we went on stage I felt just like a non-league soccer player must feel when he finds himself playing in front of managers and players from the senior leagues.

The summer brought an opportunity to get back into the circus again. Bernard Bale, a former journalist turned circus proprietor and entertainer and his partner, wild animal trainer Al Verlaine, had taken over Cleethorpes Zoo and because of their circus background, they wanted to have a circus in the park throughout the summer.

I was thrilled when Bernard asked if we would like to appear in the show. It was the time when I had a static holiday caravan at Ingoldmells, just outside Skegness and I remember spending one holiday there and commuting most days forty of so miles up the coast to Cleethorpes to take part in the show.

I used to joke we were the only circus act in the world with a caravan forty miles away from the Big Top.

The circus had a group of lions, expertly shown by Al, and I was able to appreciate at first hand the patience and dedication he showed to his animals. The only snag was the lions used to open the show and it seemed to take an eternity to dismantle the cage at the end of their act, so the rest of the performance could carry on. We were doing two spots in the show, the juggling act and an act made up of a combination of the rope-spinning and the disco ribbons.

Sadly the venture wasn't a tremendous success

and I can't ever remember seeing more than forty people in the tent for any one performance. And there was another problem too. There seemed to be so few people running the zoo and most of them appeared to be working in the circus. So once a show started I couldn't help feeling they must have lost money because there was no one around to sell sweets, ice creams and other refreshments to the visitors.

It was early June, well before the peak of the summer season, when the tent was finally dismantled, and many of the leading figures in the zoo left.

But it wasn't quite the end of our involvement with the zoo. Ken Dodd had been booked to give a show there in early July, and I suppose they couldn't cancel his contract, because on a Thursday evening his show went ahead on a raised-up stage in the open-air. Fortunately it was a dry and warm evening. What would have happened if it had been anything other doesn't bear thinking about.

But around two hundred people gathered around the stage for the show and although Ken doesn't need any sort of supporting bill, because he is capable of staying on stage for longer than anyone I have ever come across, we were booked to provide the one and only supporting act, doing twenty minutes of juggling, rope-spinning and comedy.

It wasn't the first time I had met Ken. Sometime earlier, when he had been to Lincoln to attend a police sports day, I had interviewed him for the Echo and although quite a few months must have elapsed and I was looking very different this time, he seemed to remember me from our previous meeting.

Come the autumn, I was back under the Big Top of James Brothers Circus in Wisbech. By now, the circus had grown in size and importance and if they had a Top Twenty of British circuses at the time, I suppose this one would have been somewhere around the middle.

The show was very good and Jim had recently taken delivery of a big new tent. To those with little more than a passing interest in travelling circuses, I must point out that Big Tops come in a variety of shapes and sizes. At the smallest level the canvas roof is held up by just a single king pole which generally stands slap bang in the middle of the ring. Yeldings had used a tent like this and so had Jim on occasions in the smaller towns. The big thing to remember about this kind of tent was that, if you happened to be moving backwards while you were juggling, you ran the risk of backing into the king pole.

Then there were the two-pole tents, like the one used by Bernard and Al's Circus Colossus at Cleethorpes Zoo and the one that Jim had tended to use quite a lot. These were bigger and the poles were sited at opposite ends of the ring, so you had the peace of mind of knowing you weren't going to collide with a king pole - not unless something particularly unexpected had happened.

And then there were the four pole Big Tops. These tended to have the biggest seating capacities and would stand the wind better and the ring slotted neatly in the middle of the four poles.

This was my first time working in a four-mast tent and it felt a bit like a canvas cathedral, in comparison to some of the others.

Christmas arrived at the end of the usual busy period of parties. Everyone wants entertainment on the same few days and after weeks when there doesn't seem to be very much happening, there's a hectic two or three weeks in December when you could be at two or three places every day.

That December I remember we had just about everything from pre-school play groups to the elderly and from cubs to an entire village primary school. For once we were working on Boxing Day lunchtime and it wasn't the sort of thing I particularly liked doing because, in my work at the Echo I had such little time off around Christmas, that we tried to keep some days free for the family.

But on this occasion we had been booked for a family show at a club in a Lincoln barracks. The working area was very small but that wasn't the biggest problem. The room was several storeys up in a square-shaped sort of tower and the only way of getting there was by using a staircase which wrapped itself round and round the tower.

Now, as an act we don't travel light and I have never been in the happy position of being able to afford a roadie to take my props from the car to the stage. So we must have been up and down those stairs perhaps twenty times, with armfuls of equipment and that was before we even did the hour-long show.

And at the end of that we had the task of taking everything back down again. Not for the first time in my life, have I wished that I had been a comedian or singer.

The next summer found us back at Trusville Holiday Estate again, this time every Thursday night for nineteen weeks. And I really had no alternative but to try out a lot of new material this time, because as some families stayed two weeks, it meant there were children who would see us on two occasions. Some elements in the show, like the juggling and the rope-spinning could be used every week, while others

- particularly the comedy routines and the audience participation spots - couldn't.

Of course you couldn't always win, because there were times when disappointed children would come up to us at the end of the evening and say "You didn't do the vacuum cleaner or the rock factory this week," and I would have to try to explain that we tried never to do exactly the same show two weeks running.

It was great to be working with Paul Kane again, as to many children he really was the face of Trusville and there was no doubt he was fondly-remembered by many of them from one year to the next.

We may have been taking home more money from Trusville this year but we were earning it. First we did a couple of hours party night in the dance hall. Then, when that was finished, we would load everything into the car and drive round to the adult room on the other side of the holiday village to present our juggling and rope-spinning in the club for the parents.

It would often be around eleven o'clock before we were on the way home and with work the next day at half-past eight, there must have been times when I was turning up looking just a little bit weary. Jim was just down the road from Trusville with his circus and although we couldn't join him during the summer, we did take part in a variety show he put on at a country club on the outskirts of the resort during August.

One of the acts was an attractive young girl who appeared topless with a snake. Not the sort of thing she could have done for a family audience under the Big Top but it went down very well with the adults.

With the end of the Mablethorpe season the circus took to the road again and by now I was booking most of the grounds for the show. To be honest, if I had ever found myself being in the position of owning a circus, this is the one job I would have insisted on doing myself, because when you think about it, it's the most important part of the whole lot.

After all you can have the best show in Britain but if you are in the wrong place at the wrong time, then it's a complete disaster. But, for some reason or other, Jim asked me to liaise with the local authorities, who owned most of the circus sites in those days, and book a route for the circus.

You had to know which circus had appeared in any particular town and when, because if people had gone along to the last circus and hadn't enjoyed it, then you would have the devil of a job to get them back again. You generally didn't go to anywhere within six months of the last circus. You had to be aware when the local holiday weeks were, because you didn't want the circus to arrive in a town when most of the people were away on holiday. Similarly, you had to avoid the well-established fairs, because it would have been no good the circus setting up its Big Top on the edge of a town, when the streets were filled by the annual fair.

And on top of all this you tried to avoid the circus going back to the same town two years running and you had to watch that you weren't asking the show to travel too many miles from one place to the next, because there always seemed to be a shortage of drivers and some lorries had to make every trip two-and-a-half times with different trailers in tow.

I generally used to aim for moves of around thirty miles and that seemed to work pretty well.

That autumn I had managed to negotiate the Goose Fair site in Nottingham. This had always been something of a special place for me, because as a teenager whenever a circus had visited Nottingham, it was near enough for me go ride over on my motor scooter to see it.

I had watched some of the greatest circus artistes in some of the greatest circuses appearing on the Goose Fair site and now I was appearing here myself. Somehow it didn't seem right. Although it's close on forty miles from the Echo office in Lincoln, to the circus ground in Nottingham, I managed to get over almost every day, though the five o'clock show must have been half way through by the time I arrived.

Towards the end of the month the circus was at Leicester on the Almond Road Car Park site at the cattle market. It was an excellent site in many respects and its hard surface was ideal for the late November weather. But I remember it gave the plate-spinner a few problems, because if his plates spun off the end of their rods and finished up on the ground, they would invariably smash. It wasn't like a farm field or a grass park, where they stood a chance of surviving the fall.

By the end of the stay in Leicester, he must have got through quite a few plates and left quite a bit of broken crockery behind.

Having appeared at the last place in the circus's 1979 tour, it was good to appear at the first place of the 1980 tour, which was Hearsall Common in Coventry.

But we nearly didn't make it. The show was opening on a Monday in mid-March and I had the day off work to travel down for the two performances. But when the day arrived, there was something approaching a blizzard in Lincoln and even I had to admit that it wasn't worth the risk of a lengthy drive to Coventry and back under those conditions.

By the end of the week, the weather had improved, and we went down for the three shows on the Saturday and business was good. I had a new costume in time for Coventry and it was one which was to last me for quite a long time.

Gone at last were the crushed velvet trousers and the tie top. Now I had a tailor-made red cat suit and a white satin shirt.

I have done a number of what I privately consider to be unusual things during my life and the summer of 1980 saw one of them. I hired an entire British circus - complete with two fairly large performing elephants - to the American Air Force.

I was still booking most of the grounds for Jim's circus and one place I had tried for, without success, was Huntingdon. But the council must have kept my letter on file, because some time later the American Air Force were looking for a circus for their Independence Day celebrations at the nearby Alconbury air base.

They wrote to me, asking if the circus would be available and I realised that there was time for the circus to go there for the weekend before moving up to Mablethorpe for the summer.

I was invited down to the base and ushered through the gate guards, who I noticed were carrying rifles. Security seemed to be tight. I was shown a stretch of grass right alongside of the runways. "Would that be suitable for the circus?" asked the officer accompanying me.

Before I could answer, there was a deafening roar as a fighter aircraft took to the skies.

"Well," I replied, "the site is fine but we might have a few problems with the animals every time an aircraft took off!"

But he explained, there would be no flying during the July 4th celebrations and a deal was struck.

Although the visit was mainly for the benefit of the American service personnel and their families, the general public would be allowed in as well, so the visit would have to be well advertised.

The circus was opening for three days, giving shows daily at 11.30am, 3.30p.m. and 7.30p.m. and I was taking part in all of them.

Although Jim had hired in extra seating for the visit, the tent seldom seemed to be more than a third full and July 4th itself - which I had expected to be very busy - was possibly the quietest. It was explained to me afterwards that in some respects it was like Christmas Day and most people spent the day at home having their own parties.

But straight after the last show of the day, there was a firework display which was as good as any I have seen anywhere.

With plenty of time to spare between the performances, we had an opportunity to explore the base and to get a taste of the American way of life, because the base was very much a little piece of America in the middle of Britain.

Even the circus box office had to handle American dollars. We made good use of the Ten Pin Bowling alley and I was impressed when daughter Karen, who wasn't quite eleven, showed her method of just picking up a bowl and dropping it at the end of the rink and allowing it to roll, oh so slowly, towards the pins, was almost as successful as the experts.

Our next show, just a couple of weeks later, came right out of the blue.

I was looking forward to a family holiday back in

our caravan at Ingoldmells and I had booked tickets to see The Ken Dodd Show at the old Festival Pavilion in Skegness. Just a couple of days before the show, I got a call from the promoter, asking if I would like to be in the show.

Tickets were in such demand that once I had explained the situation and said yes I would be delighted to be in the show, he then asked me to return the tickets so they could sell them again.

This really was the big time for what was still a very modest juggling and rope-spinning act. There were to be two performances on a Sunday evening. The first show, was perhaps fifty short of the 1,300 capacity and the second one was absolutely full.

The first show started at 6.20p.m. and we were the first act on. As I looked around the wings, waiting for the curtain to go up, I had a feeling that something was missing. Then I realised what it was. Ken Dodd hadn't arrived.

We went on, did our spot, came off again and still no Ken Dodd. Ward Allen, the talented ventriloquist who was on next, commented "If he doesn't turn up soon, this is going to be the shortest first-half in history."

But we needn't have worried. A few minutes later he arrived in time and soon had the audience in the palm of his hand but it must have given the promoters a few anxious moments. After all how would you explain to a near-capacity audience that the star of the show hadn't arrived?

Although I have seen Ken on stage perhaps a dozen times and had the pleasure of interviewing him either face to face or on the end of a telephone on a number of occasions, I have never seen him even remotely lost for words, until the second performance of the day at Skegness.

He was in full cry when suddenly his radio mic started picking up the signals of a nearby taxi. It took a few moments before everyone realised what was happening and then Ken was quick to take advantage of the situation.

But for a long time afterwards, I couldn't help wondering if the unfortunate taxi driver could hear everything that was going on inside the Festival Pavilion as well.

We were to appear at the Festival Pavilion a few years later with our own little Sunday afternoon children's show but if you go looking for the venue today you won't find it. Last time I was there, the site was an open piece of land at the side of the boating lake.

The building had a varied history, starting off as an open-air roller skating rink and later being roofed over. It was ideal for all kinds of things like wrestling, exhibitions and dances. It even served as an electrical factory at one time. But it wasn't particularly ideal for shows, because the stage was fairly small and the seats weren't raked, so if you weren't sitting on the first few rows, you didn't stand much of a chance of seeing what was going on.

It would have been ideal for something like an ice show or a circus, with the audience sitting all round. But as far as I know, it never served those purposes. Its eventual demolition marked the end of an era in the resort.

Chapter Eleven

Medieval Madness and a Circus Landmark

Have you ever been to a medieval banquet? I had sampled a couple at a pub in Horncastle, and thoroughly enjoyed them. So I was quite excited when I was invited to be one of the entertainers at a banquet at an ancient hotel called the Angel and Royal, in the centre of Grantham, in the autumn of 1980. The only thing that worried me a little was that I didn't possess a costume, which I considered to be strictly medieval and most of the props I used in my juggling and rope-spinning acts bore strong links to the late 20th century.

In the end I donned perhaps the most suitable clothes I could find and things seemed to work out pretty well. It was the first of two visits I was to pay to the venue in the run-up to Christmas and I had to get used to working to medieval music provided by real-live minstrels, rather than my usual disco type of records.

The audiences were the kind you didn't find in any other event. They were there to enjoy themselves, let their hair down, forget their usual table manners and enter into the whole spirit of the occasion. Audience participation was very much the thing and you never seemed to have any real difficulty in enticing people out of their seats to come and try their hand at juggling.

After the usual round of children's parties and school visits during December, there was a quiet start to the New Year, before I was back with James Brothers Circus for their opening stand of the season in Leicester once more.

The beauty of Leicester was it was within an easy drive of home, although I almost always used to fall foul of the traffic system. Like so many motorists in so many other towns and cities, I could always see exactly where I wanted to be but the traffic flows always seemed to be going in the wrong direction.

A month later the circus was at Edmonton in North London and I went down to do two shows on the Friday. The weather was atrocious and the Big Top was built up on grass at the foot of a slope. It rained and it rained and most of the water ran down the sodden grass and ended up in the circus ring, which seemed to be at the lowest point of the field.

It wasn't long before half the ring was under water and I remember the horses had to be left out of the show because they would have splashed through the puddles and sent mud and water cascading over the people sitting in the front rows.

Now, bearing in mind this was the last weekend in April, you might have thought we had seen the last of winter. But as I drove back up the A1 that night towards Lincoln, I suddenly realised I couldn't see any of the sign posts at the side of the road. Then I realised they were completely obscured by snow. By the time I reached Lincoln the ground was white over, as the heavy rain had turned to a blizzard.

During the summer a small circus arrived in the Lincoln area. It was billed as Poole Brothers Circus and the show was presented in a single-mast tent which probably held a couple of hundred people. I found I knew some of the people in the show and I was able to take part in a couple of performances, when the circus arrived at North Hykeham.

Later that summer the nation was celebrating the marriage of Prince Charles and Lady Diana, and the nation was in a party spirit. There weren't quite as many street parties and galas as there had been to mark the Queen's Silver Jubilee four years earlier, but there were enough to keep us busy for a few days and for once the weather kept fine.

One of the parties we attended was in the street where we lived in Lincoln and we did the show straight outside our own front window.

Autumn found us back with James Brothers Circus on the picturesque Embankment site at Peterborough and a couple of weeks later in a field behind a pub on the outskirts of King's Lynn. The King's Lynn visit was special for a number of reasons. It was the first time I had ever appeared in Norfolk, which was my late father's birthplace. It was the first time my young daughter, Karen, had joined me in the circus ring, and it was also my 100th performance in a circus.

Now 100 circus performances may not sound a tremendous achievement, when you bear in mind that most circuses were giving twelve or even thirteen shows every week for perhaps forty weeks a year. But you had to remember that my circus involvement was limited to days off and the occasional holiday, while fitting in a full-time job at the Lincolnshire Echo as well.

Karen was always very much into gymnastics, so it wasn't surprising that not long after she started assisting in the juggling act and disco ribbons, she was performing her own acrobatic routine as well.

The biggest difficulty she faced at many of the smaller venues was that the working area just wasn't big enough for many of her moves, and she ran the constant risk of catapulting herself into a wall or off the edge of the stage. But there was no doubt that in the places where she could work her routine added a new dimension to our show.

Most of the bookings we were getting at this time were by word-of-mouth. People would see us at one venue and invite us to go along to their child's party or to their local school at sometime in the future. But towards the end of the year an agent saw us somewhere or got to hear about us and started putting work our way.

It wasn't long before Lincoln Management and Entertainment Agency had us on their books and I have been with them ever since. Working through an agent did give you an added responsibility. Until then, if anyone hadn't been particularly keen on the show (heaven forbid), it was our own fault but when you were working through an agent you always dreaded that they would receive a bad report and immediately strike you from their books for ever.

Happily it doesn't seem to have happened yet but the fear is always in the back of your mind.

The following February found us back at Holy Trinity Church in Dalston for what was this time the 36th annual Clowns' Memorial Service and Show. The stage in the church hall was so small that there wasn't room to do some of the tricks I would usually have included in the juggling and rope-spinning routines and there was no question at all of Karen being able to do her acrobatics. A cartwheel-and-a-half and she would have been three rows back in the audience.

But I was also assisting Bimbo in his comedy camera routine. I took part in this routine several times over the years and never got tired of it, because almost every time it was different. If you have never seen anyone do the routine and you probably have at one time or another, it starts with the clown walking out onto the stage with a pretend television camera.

Bimbo would call for a volunteer - on this occasion it was me - and out I would come, delighted and flattered to have the opportunity of appearing in front of the camera. There would be some nonsense with the stool I had to sit on and if you picked it up correctly, all four legs would fall off together.

The camera had a mind of its own and, not unlike my own "exploding" vacuum cleaner, it would puff out smoke, squirt water at the victim on the receiving end, let out an ear-piercing buzz and produce a cuddly teddy bear and a flag with the word "Bang" printed in big letters on it.

Most of the script, such as it was, we made up as we went along but we always ended up enjoying ourselves and I like to think that some of the enjoyment rubbed off on the audience as well.

As usual, whenever I drove through London, I ended up getting lost on the way home. Eventually, despite the best efforts of my A to Z of London and everybody's navigation, I spotted a sign pointing out the way to the A1. At long last we were on our way home. Unfortunately what I hadn't realised was that at this point the A1 went in both directions and rather than heading northwards and out into the open countryside, we found ourselves heading south and back into the centre of London again.

It had been a very long and tiring day and the extra miles, through congested and unknown London streets on a cold and miserable Sunday night in February did little to improve how we must all have been feeling.

During the summer I was asked to do something which, at first glance, sounds a little insane. I was invited to juggle on the radio. Yes, just think about that for a moment. It does sound odd doesn't it.

The people at Eastgate Leisure Centre at Ingoldmells were having a day to raise money for charity and one of the ideas my long-time friend and public relations whiz, Geoff Barry, came up with was that in the open-air market at the centre, passersby and shoppers should be challenged to find objects I couldn't juggle with.

If their challenge failed, they would have to give a donation to the charity. If I failed, the organisers would give them a souvenir pen. Chris Jones from BBC Radio Lincolnshire was there to describe to listeners just what was going on.

Now, I have always made a point of using a lot of very different props in my juggling routine. I knew a lot of jugglers specialised in clubs, bean bags, rings or even chainsaws and they were far better than I could ever hope to be.

So what I did was to use a large variety of, sometimes unusual, props, in the hope that audiences wouldn't realise that I was not particularly brilliant with any of them. And so far, I seem to have got away with it.

My usual routine would include sweeping brushes, a cricket bat and balls, tennis rackets, plates among the usual clubs, bean bags and rings. In later years I would add empty Coke cans, hammers, impressive-looking, if not particularly sharp, knives and, much later, three mobile phones.

So, if nothing else, I was fairly adept at coping with props of unusual shapes and sizes and this must have stood me in good stead on that July day at

Ingoldmells. I managed three unbreakable pint glasses, coins, toy cars, Polo mints, Oxo cubes, shoes, bottle tops even three sausages and three chips. And, bearing in mind there was a fairly strong wind blowing in off the seafront, which was guaranteed to play havoc with anything you attempted to juggle with outside, I was feeling fairly pleased with myself.

What I couldn't cope with and I don't mind at all admitting this, were cigarettes, coat hangers, wooden forks, toy windmills and baskets.

It was all good fun. No reputations were going to be made or lost that day and the little stunt even raised a few pounds for the charity.

A few days later we were back at James Brothers Circus in Mablethorpe and I think it was one of my proudest moments when Karen and Tracey, who had recently arrived at the circus, teamed up together to do a gymnastic act under the name of The Acro Sisters. I didn't know whether to watch their routine or the faces of the audience and when I heard the applause at the end of the routine, I must admit there was just a hint of a tear in the corner of my eye.

People occasionally ask if there have been any embarrassing moments in my years as a juggler, in the same way as there were during my years as a journalist. And until a Monday evening in early August 1982, I would have probably said no.

Then something happened to change all that. To set the scene, I must explain that whenever the ringmaster announced my act, I would run as fast as I could through the curtains and aim to reach the middle of the ring before the applause stopped. It couldn't have been any more than twenty feet but there was nothing worse than the applause petering out before you started.

There weren't that many people in the audience and I knew there wouldn't be a lot of applause. So the moment I heard the announcement, I ran through the curtain - indian clubs in my hand - at a speed which would have been a credit to an Olympic sprinter. What I hadn't realised was there was a small patch of mud just the other side of the curtain. I hit it, at tremendous speed, went head over heels, somehow landed back on my feet with my clubs still in my hands and tried to carry on as if nothing had happened.

Thinking about it afterwards, it was probably a good trick but it was one I was never tempted to repeat. In future, I would always take a peep through the curtains to make sure there were no unexpected hazards between there and the centre of the ring.

Although most of our shows at private parties took place in church halls, schools or village halls, there were occasions when the parties were held in private houses. And this provided me with a bit of a challenge.

Sometimes, if the parties were in the garden or in a double garage, it wasn't so bad. The most difficult thing was working to an audience of perhaps no more than a dozen children in somebody's front room. The last thing I wanted was to sweep a load of expensive ornaments off somebody's sideboard with a spinning rope, or leave a big mark on someone's lounge ceiling where one of my juggling props had hit it.

Occasionally a far-seeing parent had gone to the trouble of stripping the room of furniture entirely for the party but house parties still remain one of the biggest challenges I face and there are quite a few tricks I would never attempt under those circumstances.

When I look back through my diary and I look at some of the names of the children whose fifth, sixth and seventh birthday parties I was doing in the early 1980s, it's a sobering thought to realise that in all probability these children have grown up into adults with young children of their own.

As regular visitors to Skegness, I had watched with interest as much of the old Embassy Ballroom on Grand Parade had been demolished and a big new concert auditorium built onto the back of it. Then, with the venue not long open, I had the opportunity of being the first juggling act to appear there.

The South Lincolnshire Magicians Society was holding a Gala Night with Johnny Hillyard and Clifford Davis topping the bill. It was a memorable evening and once again I had the chance to juggle on the radio as the programme was recorded for broadcast to Lincoln hospital patients and staff. It was also at this show, that Karen had the distinction of being the first performer at the new Embassy Centre, to hurt herself during a show, when she suffered an injury in her gymnastics spot.

By this time we had left Lincoln to move to Welton. The village had, and still has, a strong and successful twinning link with a village called Monce in France and we were invited to go to the cabaret in our village hall when a group of Monce children arrived on an exchange visit.

Luckily it wasn't essential that I spoke the language, because, as I have mentioned before, foreign languages aren't my thing. However, just to show willing, I had spent several weeks rehearsing how to offer a warm welcome to our French visitors. Day in and day out, I would run through those same few words in my head, until I felt reasonably sure I had got the phrase exactly right.

My pronunciation might have left a lot to be desired but at least I was satisfied the words were correct. And at the end of thirty minutes on stage, I came off having felt things hadn't gone too badly, only to realise with a shock that I had never said my well-rehearsed greeting.

I don't know whether it was divine retribution or not but a few days later - while we were away on holiday - our house was hit by lightning and it started a fire which caused something like £8,000 damage. Fortunately none of my props or costumes were damaged. If I had lost them all, I would have been faced with a job of renewing and replacing them all fairly quickly, because we had a reasonable amount of work lined up that summer, including a return visit to Trusville.

Until shortly before Christmas 1983 most of the music which accompanied my shows was provided by records. Unless there were live musicians present or a disco which was prepared to play my records for me, I generally found I had to unplug my modest little stereo system from my living room at home, load the deck and speakers into my car, and use them. The volume was loud enough to fill a small hall or even a reasonably large one.

It did, of course, mean I didn't have the use of a microphone, so I had to rely on voice power alone to make myself heard.

But in the run-up to Christmas with four hundred shows under my belt - or should that be "under my catsuit"? - I decided to transfer all my music to tape and lashed out on a new tape recorder.

Later generations would probably call it a "ghetto blaster" but I will always think of it as a rather large tape recorder. I remember standing in the electrical shop in Lincoln city centre and asking the assistant: "How loud will it play?"

He gave me a strange sort of look, turned the volume up as high as it would go and every conversation in the store came to an abrupt halt as everybody looked to see where the noise was coming from.

Yes, I decided, that would probably be loud enough for my purposes and I bought it. More than twenty years later it is still doing valiant service, although now the sounds it produces are pumped out through a very ancient speaker. But more of that later on.

We were being asked to do more and more games and dances, in addition to an hour-long circus show at many children's parties in those days and one game that I came up with, I was doing at this stage. And I must admit, at the time, I was rather proud of it.

If you are of a certain generation, you will remember Derek Batey's long-running television quiz show, Mr. and Mrs. He would ask the husband questions about his wife, while she was out of earshot somewhere and then he would call the wife back to see how many questions the husband had got right. Then the situation would be reversed and it usually produced some very funny results.

Would the same sort of thing work with an audience which was predominantly children? I decided to give it a try but not as Mr. and Mrs., of course but as Brother and Sister.

You asked them fairly basic questions like: "What's your sister's favourite subject at school?", "Is her idea of a great day out a trip to the seaside, a trip to the zoo or a day round the shops?" or "What's the programme your brother really hates watching on television?"

It was uncanny, how often the answer to that last question would be Emmerdale Farm.

Using three couples, you could get the best part of thirty minutes out of a maximum of eighteen questions and generally a good time was had by all, even though there weren't some very tremendous prizes at stake.

Then there was the "Yes No Interlude" where you asked children some quick-fire questions for a minute and if they answered "Yes" or "No" to any of them, then they were out of the game.

Other games I tended to use during this period were music based, like Musical Penny. When the music stopped, children had to go to one side of the room or the other. One side of the room was "heads" and the other side was "tails". When everyone had chosen a side, I tossed a coin and if it came down "heads" then all the children on that side of the room were out. If it came down "tails" then all the children on the other side of the room were out and you could keep that going until you found a winner.

The biggest problem was if all the children decided to go to the same side of the room, then the game would come to an end very quickly. There was Musical Bridge, where the children had to walk, hop, bunny hop or run across an invisible bridge and if the music stopped when they were on the bridge then they were out.

I found that this sort of thing worked far better than musical statues, when it always seemed to be open for discussion about whether a particular child had blinked an eye or not and there was always the likelihood of a child who had been voted out of the game, quietly joining in again a few rounds later. No wonder the games sometimes seemed to go on for hours.

Another game I tended to use in my circus show was something called "Circus School". You needed about half-a-dozen children and after finding out a little about them all, you showed them how to take a bow, before coming on to the real part of the game, which was basically drawing a clown's face on a balloon, using a felt tip pen.

To find the winner you involved the audience by getting them to applaud the one they considered was the best. You could get probably five minutes out of a routine like this. Any longer, then it dragged for those who weren't taking part. Sometimes, the young artist would press down on the balloon too hard and it would burst but it all added to the fun and all the children could take their surviving balloons home at the end.

I remember one little girl's birthday party, we were doing at the White Hart Hotel in Lincoln, on New Year's Day 1984, when I suddenly realised there was an unexpected but very familiar visitor standing by the door, watching the show. Actor Robin Askwith, still fondly remembered from his cheeky roles in the Confessions films, must have been staying in the hotel while he was appearing at the Theatre Royal and he paused to see what was going on at the party.

Chapter Twelve

The Night it all Went Wrong

Sometimes the routines went horribly wrong. You knew it was all going to go horribly wrong, but there was just nothing you could do to prevent it.

One of those times came when we were doing a birthday party for a five-year-old at a club at R.A.F. Scampton, an air base just north of Lincoln. In the war, the base was famous for being the home of No 617 Dambusters Squadron, and in more recent times, it has become the base of the R.A.F. aerobatic team, The Red Arrows.

The show seemed to be going well and towards the end we did a routine called "The Ghost Entrée". This started with my partner slipping out through a door behind me, running down a semi-darkened corridor to the room at the bottom which we were using as a dressing room. While I picked up what was intended to look like a very ancient book and began trying to convince the children that the book was all about the very room we were in and how it was supposed to be haunted, my partner was frantically putting on a skeleton mask and cladding herself with a long white sheet and a white hood, before running back up the corridor to step out behind me and give me a shock.

Unfortunately on this occasion it wasn't me who got the shock. As I began reading from the book about this horrible ghost, I noticed a little girl in the audience - she couldn't have been more than five years old -

get up and walk through the door behind me, obviously on her way down the semi-darkened corridor to visit the toilet.

There was no way I could stop her, so I just had to hope she would be clear of the corridor before my partner returned as the ghost. But of course she wasn't. They must have almost bumped into one another in the semi-dark corridor and all I heard was this ear-piercing scream and footsteps running back up the corridor as the girl burst through the door back into the room in floods of tears.

It took several minutes before she could be convinced that there were are no such things as ghosts… or perhaps there are!

The summer of 1984 found Jimmy's circus back at Mablethorpe again and by now he had changed the name of the show from James Brothers Circus to Jimmy Fossett's Circus. Because the ground in Seaholme Road wasn't particularly large, he was having to use a two-pole version of his four-pole tent, and because of our other commitments we weren't able to spend quite so much time with the show that summer as we had done in the past.

The circus business has changed so much since the mid-1980s, and perhaps the biggest change of them all has come about in communication. If any business needed to welcome the arrival of mobile phone with open arms, then it's the circus and fairground world.

Before the mobile era, if you had wanted to get an urgent message to someone with a circus or fair, then you had to ring the police station in the nearest town and see if you could prevail on a kind-hearted officer to take round a message by hand. Clearly you couldn't ask him to do it for something trivial, so you generally had to make up a story about how some aged relative had been taken ill suddenly.

The circus ground at Mablethorpe had the boon of two or three public telephone kiosks at the gate and I suspect Jim had some children hanging around the boxes permanently because if ever you needed to talk to him, you just rang one of those kiosks and a youngster would answer, only too willing to take a message to "the man in the big caravan near the gate".

How mobile phones have changed all that.

Autumn brought a rather different booking for me. It was through an agent I had never worked for in the past, so I was anxious to impress. A new night spot was opening in Nottingham. As I remember, it looked as if someone had bought all the property in a small cul-de-sac and knocked it into one big venue.

On the opening night they wanted a selection of circus acts to work on the pavement outside to entertain the crowds as they waited to go in. Because the night club seemed to occupy the whole of the little street, there was very good security outside and at no time did I feel I was in any sort of danger.

Fortunately I was the only juggler booked for the evening, which was a great relief because I always hated finding myself booked alongside other jugglers. I don't mind if they are better than me but what I don't like is if they are better than me and younger than I am. And I was beginning to find that jugglers were getting younger all the time.

The great advantage with being predominantly a children's entertainer is that more often than not you are on the way home by seven o'clock at night. Not like some of the musicians and disco disc jockeys who can be hard at it until the early hours, and then face a lengthy drive back home. But with the Nottingham booking I didn't finish until ten o'clock, which must have meant it was getting on for midnight before I got home and I still had to be at my desk in the Echo office soon after eight o'clock the following morning.

At around this time I decided our circus show needed another act and I found exactly what I was looking for in one of the show business papers. Someone was selling the props for a plate-spinning act. The address was somewhere in Leamington Spa, which was a fair old drive on a Sunday afternoon but accompanied by my friend Bimbo, we drove down and I ended up buying the props.

And what a good investment they turned out to be, although as acts went it wasn't without its problems. The props consist of three wooden bases each containing four slender poles with a point on the end. The idea is you try to spin twelve plates on the top of the poles at the same time, while juggling with three plates at the end.

It can be a very fast act but it's fraught with problems because the plates, if they happen to spin off the poles, fall five or six feet to the ground and invariably smash, sending a shower of broken crockery all over the heads of the people sitting on the front row. It's also a routine which can't be worked on the smallest of stages because each of the three bases which support the uprights is six foot long.

But in the places where it can be used, it can look pretty impressive. The act was initially performed by my partner, with me handing her the plates. And it didn't take me long to realise we were getting through far too many plates. After we had used up all the spare plates I had at home, I began what became a regular search of the local charity shops trying to buy up more.

One night, after it all went badly wrong on stage at the Galaxy Suite at Ingoldmells, I decided the time had come to experiment with plastic plates. They worked for a while but the biggest drawback was that they weren't heavy enough to give a really long spin. So I bought the heaviest plastic plates I could find and even glued them together to give added weight. But it still wasn't enough and in the end I discovered enamel plates in a Lincoln camping shop. I immediately bought a dozen of them and I have never looked back, as they say.

The plates are almost as heavy as real ones and when they fall they land on the ground with the sort of noise that makes the people on the front row jump with shock. But they never break and everyone is safe and secure.

After a while, my partner decided the plate-spinning act wasn't for her, so I took it over and I have been doing it ever since.

In the run-up to Christmas 1984, I appeared at one of the most unusual venues ever. It was in the small East Lincolnshire market town of Spilsby, where the former Magistrates Court building has been turned into an attractive little theatre. The dressing rooms are the converted cells and although the place doesn't have a very large seating capacity, there is loads of atmosphere.

The reason for my appearance there was to appear at a medieval banquet.

Most of the bookings we received, particularly through the agent, were often weeks if not months in advance. But there was one really last-minute one that cropped up a few days later.

I was actually about to go on stage at a children's party in R.A.F. Digby near Sleaford, when the agent rang to see if I could go on to a show in Worksop as soon as I had finished.

It was a bit of a journey but I was able to do it, although I almost wished I hadn't.

This was the time of the miners strike and one of the printing unions had decided to sponsor a party for seven hundred and fifty youngsters in the town's Miners Welfare building.

By any stretch of the imagination, this was a big party and I think it had been running throughout most of the day. It was certainly gone seven o'clock by the time I arrived and although they had been entertained by a whole host of performers during the afternoon, it had just gone on for too long. To say the children were restless, would be to put it mildly and I think I was quite relieved when I had finished my thirty-minute spot and it was the turn of another unfortunate act to go on.

It is never very easy when you find yourself booked for two or even three appearances on the same day, especially if each of them is scheduled for the best part of an hour. You have to allow plenty of time to take costumes on and off, load equipment back into the car, do the journey, unload, set up the stage and start all over again.

You only just need to be a few minutes late starting at the first one, to be running very short of time by the end of the afternoon.

It's maybe a mixture of youth and inexperience, combined with an element of greed, that makes you do it. When I look back now at the first Saturday of January 1985, for instance, I wonder how on earth we did it. We started off with a forty-five minute spot in the social club of a hospital at Bracebridge Heath on the south side of Lincoln, at 2.15p.m. By four o'clock we were appearing at a children's party on the north side of Lincoln and ninety minutes later we were at a Sunday school party in a village eight miles to the west.

Fortunately, or unfortunately depending on how you look at it, that sort of thing doesn't happen very often. At around this time Karen joined us in the show again, this time presenting a different version of her acrobatic routine. This one was based on modern rhythmic gymnastics and could be performed in less space than her original routine.

It also seemed to me, as a relieved father, that there were fewer opportunities for her to injure herself.

I appeared at a lovely venue that spring, with the Cranwell Little Theatre Company in their pantomime Cinderella. The building was the magnificent Whittle Hall at R.A.F. College Cranwell. The backstage accommodation may not have been anything to write home about, but the auditorium and the stage were magnificent and it really gave you a good feeling to appear there.

Unfortunately, although the auditorium would have seated several hundreds in absolute comfort, the biggest of the three audiences we played to only just reached triple figures.

Appearing once more with an amateur company did bring home to me the biggest difference between amateurs and professionals. It doesn't come during the performances, because in my humble opinion some of the very gifted amateurs can be every bit as good as professionals. But the real difference comes back stage. In an amateur production, the men go into one dressing room and the women go into another. With professionals, unless you are the sort of star who commands his or her own dressing room, everyone seems to get changed together and it doesn't feel at all strange or odd.

That Spring Bank Holiday we were booked to appear in the arena at a gala in a very attractive village just outside Gainsborough and I was just a little bit worried, because the second thirty-minute spot we were doing, was identical to the first. I didn't have a huge range of routines which I could do successfully in the wide open spaces of a gala arena, so I had hoped one crowd of people would watch the first spot, and then a totally different crowd would watch the second show. And nobody would realise I was doing the same thing twice.

But of course it didn't happen. As the time was approaching for my second show of the afternoon, I realised the same people were still sitting around the arena and I was getting more and more anxious. At almost the last minute I was saved from any embarrassment when the heavens opened and it started to pour down. Everybody made a dash for home and they never came back. The gala finished abruptly with me telling the organisers how very sorry I was not to have been able to do my second spot, because it was all totally different from the first.

The next few bookings were all in the shelter of tents. First I was able to spend a couple of days back with Jim's circus when he built his two-pole Big Top in a field at North Hykeham and towards the end of the week I was appearing in a medieval banquet in a tent at a village just south of Newark.

Although it was a village steeped in history, I couldn't help thinking a marquee was not quite right for a medieval banquet but everyone seemed to enjoy themselves. My biggest problem was that the rows of tables and seats were so close together, there was hardly any room to walk up and down juggling.

As I mentioned earlier, I was no longer doing talent contests by this time but I was invited to take part in a couple of special things at Ingoldmells that summer. The first was "The Busker and Street Entertainer of the Year" contest. I didn't really consider I came into either category but I think they must have been short of acts, because I was judged winner of the speciality act section.

A couple of days later at the same venue I was given the Lincolnshire Clubland Award for the top speciality act working on the coast that summer. Again, no false modesty here but I can only think there weren't that many speciality acts working the coast that summer.

To help promote it all I was invited to do a brief stunt for Yorkshire Television in the open-air market at the venue. I was required to juggle with three eggs from one of the market stalls and although there is nothing at all difficult about this - as long as you remember not to squeeze the eggs too tightly - I was told to drop one of the eggs onto the ground so they could film it smashing everywhere.

Being television, quite a few eggs were littering the ground by the time the director was happy about the shot, and despite something like ten minutes filming, the scene occupied no more than ten seconds when it appeared on television that night.

Now, I have mentioned how difficult it is to fit three performances in during one day. In September 1985 I managed to do eleven, and it is a record that I never expect I will beat.

It started off at one o'clock when I took part in a carnival procession, juggling through the grounds of a hospital at Bracebridge Heath. For the next three hours I was taken from ward to ward doing shows of between eight and twelve minutes to patients who just weren't well enough to go down to the sports field for the carnival.

When that finished, soon after five o'clock, I was back home to get ready for a forty-mile drive to Ingoldmells, where I was due on stage at ten o'clock for the finals of the Busker and Street Entertainer competition.

I don't know who it was who once told me "fire impresses" but it was a circus entertainer and he was absolutely right.

Once you introduce fire into any sort of performance, whether it's juggling or fire-eating, it seems to command instant respect.

I had been wanting to bring in fire juggling as a finale to my act for a long time and I had the opportunity when I was in Bromley that summer and bought a set of three fire torches from a shop at the Churchill Theatre.

The first task, in the privacy of my own home, was to juggle with the torches unlit. It was no more difficult than juggling with Indian clubs. So out in the back garden, I coated one of the torches with paraffin and lit it. When I had plucked up courage I tossed it from one hand to the other and discovered that it made a satisfactory swishing noise as it flew through the air. The next step was to juggle with the other two unlit torches at the same time.

Gradually, as my confidence and courage increased, I began to realise just how little or how much paraffin was needed to produce a satisfactory flame and eventually I had all three torches lit and was juggling them with ease. Obviously I have never been able to rehearse this trick inside my house, so any practising that was needed, had to be done on my back lawn, where hopefully not too many of the neighbours would have been able to see.

My first attempt at juggling my fire torches in public was in the grounds of Lincoln Castle on a Sunday in October. Working on my own and clad in red crushed velvet trousers and tie top - so I must have been a bit chilly around the middle - I spent four-and-a-half hours at a Scouts Medieval Activity Day. There were processions, walk-rounds and some entertainment to do inside a marquee.

As I remember, the weather wasn't ideal with strong winds and occasional showers, so I must have been quaking a bit as I lit my fire torches for the first time. But the effect was everything I had hoped it would be and from that moment the fire torches were in my show and they were there to stay.

There was an abundance of children's parties in the run-up to Christmas but you got the impression that even the biggest factories and organisations in the area didn't have as much money to spend even on children's entertainment as they once had.

We were being asked to do more and more on stage as the organisers didn't have the money to employ more than one entertainer. In a bid to extend our show, without adding too much to the amount of props I was stuffing into the boot of my car every time we went out, I came up with a new routine which I called the Japanese Miracle Box.

It was just a normal cardboard box and I would get a child in the audience to write his or her name on a note pad, with the promise that I would draw a card bearing the same name, from inside the Japanese Miracle Box. What I didn't tell them was it would be a Japanese word which I would try to convince them was their name in Japanese.

Karen was going to night school for Japanese at the time. She has always had a far greater grasp of foreign languages than I have and she wrote the word "Hello" in authentic Japanese on the card. I hadn't wanted to run the risk of drawing a few squiggles on the card and waving it about a room full of children, only to discover at some later date that I had written something rather rude in Japanese, quite by chance.

I shall always be eternally grateful to a store called Titan Trading for putting some work my way in 1986. They had several branches in the North of England and at Easter they hit on this idea of holding a family day, in the hope that mums and dads would bring their children along to be entertained and they would go off and buy a three-piece suite or something.

Easter Monday found us in their Huddersfield store doing a couple of twenty-minute shows to reasonably-sized audiences, in a space on the first floor. It was the first time I had ever appeared in Yorkshire and I spent around three hours walking round the store, juggling and spinning ropes, and generally chatting to staff and customers.

There was no pressure and the money wasn't bad, so when the firm asked me to do something similar at their store in Preston a week or so later, I was only too pleased to accept. But as it turned out, this was one of the few bookings I wasn't able to fulfill. The windscreen wiper motor in my car burned out and I just couldn't get it repaired in time for the long journey across the Pennines to Preston. It would have been unthinkable to drive all that way with no windscreen wipers especially as it was a pretty wet day. Although the company was very understanding about it, I still regret being unable to travel to Preston.

I think Titan Trading must have forgiven me because over the May Day Bank Holiday I was back at their Huddersfield store once again doing the same thing as before and, although there were fewer people around, I had the fun of juggling live on Pennine Radio which was doing an outside broadcast from the store.

Later in the summer I did a similar promotion one evening at the company's store in Lincoln but most of the holiday season we seemed to spend on the Lincolnshire coast, which gave me the opportunity to make good use of my static caravan which was still parked at Ingoldmells. On most Saturday evenings during July and August I was appearing at a new venue called Panda's Palace in Skegness. Although you get indoor playgrounds like it more or less all over the country nowadays, Panda's Palace was something of a forerunner. At half-past eight on a Saturday night we would clear the mini-dodgem cars off their little track, assemble our props and do a twenty-minute show, hopefully keeping the children happy while their parents spent some money at the café.

Sunday evenings would find us at Coastfield Holiday Camp, which was just a stone's throw or two from where my own caravan was parked. Then, after the show on Sunday evening, I would drive back home in time to go into work at half-past eight the next morning.

It was while we were appearing at Coastfield that I notched up my 500th performance.

Towards the end of the summer, in what was to be my final stint with Titan Trading at Lincoln, I did a show of fifteen minutes to just three children. It was one of seven short shows I did throughout the day and having persuaded the three youngsters that the show was just about to start and keeping them waiting in the vain hope that others would turn up, I didn't have the heart to tell them to go away again.

So I did the whole thing for three and believe me, it was one of the most difficult ones I have ever done.

Sometimes when you are doing outdoor shows, your biggest difficulty is finding somewhere to change. Just occasionally I have been known to strip off at the side of my car or behind a tent but at Epworth Show that August Bank Holiday, I had to change inside a Punch and Judy booth. It may have been cramped but I would have been in a bad way without it.

Sometimes working outdoors can pose unexpected problems as well and you can't help thinking they could only happen in rural Lincolnshire. In the late summer of 1986 I was mid-way through my routine at a hospital gala near Lincoln, when a Spitfire and a Hurricane roared low overhead. They must have been on their way back to the Battle of Britain Memorial Flight Museum at Coningsby and spotting the crowd, decided to treat them to an unexpected show, without realising there was an act in full swing down at ground level.

There was no way I could compete with an aerial display, so I stopped what I was doing and gave a running commentary on what was going on above our heads, filling in any gaps with what little information I knew about Second World War fighter aircraft. I just hoped that I had correctly identified which was the Spitfire and which was the Hurricane. But I had a 50-50 chance and nobody came up to me afterwards and said I was wrong, so luck must have been on my side.

When the aircraft had roared away again, I carried on with the show as though the whole thing had been planned.

Chapter Thirteen

The Burning Question

By now, I had plucked up enough courage to use my fire torches regularly in the show, although I still had to pick and choose my venues. I wasn't, for instance, ever going to light them up at a pre-school playgroup or at a party where most of the children were under four. Nor was I ever going to use them where I was within a few feet of the people sitting on the front row.

But I had no hesitation in using them for the outdoor shows.

One question people often ask is do I ever get burned? Strange as it may seem, I have yet to catch the fire torches at the wrong end. If I did, I imagine I would let them go pretty quickly. Occasionally, if there is a strong wind blowing, I have been known to singe the hairs on my arm or on the back of my hand, and my greatest fear is that I am one day going to find I have set my clown wig on fire. But, touch wood, it hasn't happened yet.

I very seldom drop the fire torches on stage, although there was one occasion when I was doing a birthday party in a village chapel, where a very worried organiser watched as I set out the stage and uttered the fateful words: "You will be very careful, won't you. We have just had a new carpet laid."

From the moment the words left her lips I just knew I was going to drop a fire torch and of course I did. But because flames burn upwards, there was never any danger of the torches setting the carpet alight.

When I did a charity concert at Lincoln Theatre Royal that autumn, I used my fire torches and it was only sometime afterwards that I discovered a couple of people were standing in the wings with buckets of water, just in case I accidentally set the curtains alight. Whether or not they would have doused me with water, I never did find out, because the worst never happened. When you consider that once, during its memorable history, the theatre was almost totally destroyed by fire, you can perhaps realise the reason for the sensitivity.

But whether or not that fire was caused by a juggler, I have never been able to discover.

That Christmas there was a very special venue for me, because among the bookings we had was one at St. Peter-in-Eastgate Infants School, where I had been a pupil from five to seven years old. It was wonderful to go back there again and to watch the children enjoying the show, just as I would have done getting on for forty years earlier.

In my quest to constantly keep adding routines and acts to my show, I have from time to time tried out new things, which have subsequently turned out to be complete and utter disasters.

Among the many things I have never been able to do successfully are to ride a unicycle and to balance on a roller board. Perhaps the biggest problem people face in learning how to ride a unicycle, is to actually find someone who will sell them one. I once found a man in a village not far from Lincoln, who made unicycles. They weren't that difficult to ride, he assured me. In fact, there were times when he rode all the way into Lincoln and back on one.

So I duly parted with £25 and proudly carried home the purchase, which was to add a whole new dimension to my show. I had seen a unicyclist in a show, sometime ago, doing a routine whereby he rode around obstacles on the floor and ended up juggling with them.

The ideal place to practice was in the corridor at the foot of the stairs in our house. If I lost my balance I could jump off forward or backwards and if I fell to either side the walls would give me some support.

The days turned into weeks. The weeks became months and I was still no nearer mastering the wretched machine. But what I was getting were some very nasty bruises on the inside of the tops of my legs, which was just about the only part of your body with which you could grip the cycle seat.

In the end, I had to admit defeat, and gave the unicycle away.

My attempts to become a roller balancer were even more disastrous. I remembered watching the roller balancers on Jim's circus, and they had made it all look so easy. Again, if I could successfully do something like they did, it would add a whole new dimension to my show.

In case you can't visualise what a roller balancer does, he places a reasonably large tube on the ground, balances a short piece of wood across it like a seasaw and then stands on it. Once he has achieved that minor miracle, he can then do a variety of things like balancing objects on his hands and head, or threading his body through a series of hoops.

My first problem was getting the right equipment. In the end my tube was a good solid piece of metal drainpipe. I carefully placed a suitable piece of wood across it and eased myself into the standing position.

When I had mustered enough courage, I let go of the wall I had been clinging on to. I did a few wobbles, managed to stand almost upright for a fraction of a second. Then the board shot off one way, I shot off the other and I was convinced I had broken my hip.

Luckily the only thing that was damaged was my pride and I never went back onto my roller board again.

During the summer of 1987, we accompanied Bimbo to London for a Variety Club of Great Britain Sunshine Coach Rally in Hyde Park. It was a huge occasion. A couple of circus tents were built up near the centre of the park. Most of the day, we were to spend mixing and mingling with the hundreds of children and then during the afternoon we were to do a spot in front of an audience of a couple of hundred in a circus tent.

Being a Variety Club event, there were celebrities galore and I remember meeting the now late Roy Castle in the parade and rubbing shoulders with people like Clare Rayner. The only snag was the high level of security. We had to park in an underground car park at Hyde Park and then carry everything right through the park.

I don't travel light and by the time I had walked backwards and forwards between the car and the tent, I was pretty well shattered, also bearing in mind we had been up at some ungodly hour and I had driven more than 130 miles down to London. And after six hours on our feet, it was time for the long trek back to the car park again, arms full of props and costumes and then drive another 130 miles back up the A1 to Lincoln.

But seeing the smiles on the faces of the youngsters and the joy of knowing that you had in some small way contributed to a very worthwhile cause, somehow seemed to make it all worth while.

Later that summer we appeared at a lovely venue in Huddersfield. It was an open air theatre in Greenhead Park. We were booked for two twenty-minute spots and in the belief that after one audience had seen the first show they would then get up and go away, allowing a totally different audience to come in and see us doing the second show, I had planned to do almost exactly the same thing all over again.

Unfortunately it didn't take me long to realise the audience wasn't going anywhere. It was a lovely day and they were quite content to sit around the stage waiting for us to come back again. This time the rain wasn't going to save us, so between spots I desperately had to think of ways we could vary the show and do different things with the props I had available. Although some elements had to remain the same, like the juggling and rope-spinning and Karen's acrobatics, we were able to do enough other variations to keep everyone happy.

During the run-up to Christmas we were booked for a playgroup party in a little village just over the Nottinghamshire border. We did the show and a few games and then a minor disaster happened. Someone discovered they had forgotten to book a Santa. Sixty children were waiting excitedly for the great man to arrive but now it looked as if he wasn't coming.

Being a playgroup the whole thing was run by women and I was the only man around. So when they asked if I could stand in for the real Santa, I had no alternative. We still had an hour or two to spare before our next booking of the day, a Christmas market in the streets of Gainsborough. So I donned the Santa suit, covered my face with cotton wool and arrived to great cheers from the children.

But I couldn't help thinking I must have been the skinniest and possibly the youngest Santa they had ever seen.

That Christmas we had a few days off so it was arranged we would go to a hotel in Torquay. We were part of a coach party and the organiser knew what I did in my spare time, so on an evening when there was a gap in the entertainment programme, I was asked to do a short spot.

Now being a juggler and rope-spinner isn't like being a singer or a comedian. Under similar circumstances, they can get away with a few songs and telling the odd joke or two. But with me, most of my act is worked around props and you just don't take three fire torches, three tennis rackets, an assortment of clubs, rings and bean bags and all the rest of it, on holiday with you - especially not if you are travelling by coach.

So I had to improvise juggling with just about anything and everything the hotel could provide easily. The act consisted of juggling with an assortment of cutlery and plastic tumblers but at least in the years to come I could proudly boast that I had appeared in Torquay.

The words "medieval banquet" came back into my vocabulary again a few weeks later, when I was asked to take part in a couple at the former R.A.F. base at Manby near Louth. This time I hired a jester's costume and I must admit I did feel more the part this time, although many of my props still belonged firmly in modern times.

During the evening we threw out what they called "Peter's Challenge", where the diners were invited to find things I couldn't juggle with. We had done this sort of thing before but being a medieval banquet everybody was in good spirits and among the objects I was offered (and successfully juggled with) were a bra, a pair of pants and a suspender belt! I didn't enquire too deeply about where they had come from, but some of the items were still warm.

After another return to the Clowns International Show at Holy Trinity Church Hall in Dalston, the next show provided an interesting challenge. I have never been fortunate enough or perhaps never been good enough to be offered the chance of doing cabaret on a cruise ship. But at least I had the next best thing on Valentine's Day 1988.

We had been booked for a children's birthday party. But this one wasn't taking place in a private house, or a village hall or a social club. Her parents had hired the pleasure boat which used to take visitors from Brayford Pool in the centre of Lincoln and down the old Fossdyke canal.

After the children had eaten, the boat would be moored a mile or two outside the city, while we did a show. The biggest problem here was the lack of space, and the ceiling was so low that an adult could hardly stand upright. But somehow we managed to do a fifty-minute show which included an element of juggling - although on this occasion I thought it best not to attempt to use the fire torches.

During the summer ITV was staging one of its Telethon appeals to raise money for good causes and somehow - I can't remember now how it came about - but I got roped in. I was supposed to juggle in Castle Hill, in the historic heart of Lincoln. It was a wonderful setting for television because on one side you had the magnificent West Front of the cathedral and on the other side you had the walls and the main gate to the Norman castle.

But sadly what it didn't have on that Friday morning in April, were many people. So someone took the decision that we would move everything down to City Square, a raised paved area between the Central Market and the River Witham. After spending quite a lot of time making complete fools of ourselves in front of the lunchtime shoppers, the action then switched to the Echo office where I was filmed at my desk doing my everyday job.

Unfortunately, despite all the effort, as far as I could discover the item was never screened.

We had more luck with Central Television a few months later. Thanks to an agent in Nottingham, we landed some extra work in a programme called Hard Cases. It was set in a prison and starred Kevin McNally as a probation officer, who was held hostage by the prisoners during a riot. The International Community Centre in Mansfield Road - not far from where I used to go to college to learn all about how to be a journalist - became the prison.

I was cast as a prisoner, although I flatly refused to have my long curly hair trimmed and my partner and Karen were cast as prison visitors. The money was far better than just about anything we were earning doing the shows in those days. We didn't need any props and we didn't have to supply our own costumes.

We were taken in a coach out on location and we were fed and watered. It was a complete doddle. We spent most of the time sitting around, talking to the other extras and I think I was involved in just four short scenes. My partner and Karen had to do even less.

What I couldn't help noticing was that once we

had been fitted out in our costumes - we prisoners in one set of clothing and the men who were playing the prison officers in their uniform - we immediately divided ourselves into two groups. No one told us to and we didn't do it deliberately. It just happened. The prisoners automatically went one side of the room and the prison officers went to the other.

And we stayed like that for the rest of the day. What the people in the streets must have thought, when they saw all these convicts go by in a coach, I can't imagine. They must have thought the local prison was having a day out or something.

We had to wait almost exactly a year to see ourselves on screen and I noted I was in view for just fifteen seconds but it was surprising just how many people we knew spotted us.

One thing I learned during my early days is that no matter if there aren't many people about, if you are in costume and you are meant to be working, then you behave exactly as you would if there were hundreds watching you intently. And it paid off during the autumn of 1988. One of Lincoln's biggest nightspots was having a gala re-opening after a massive facelift and we were booked among the entertainers who would perform on the pavement outside the front door.

I must admit I wasn't too happy about doing it because it meant working the street in the city centre after ten o'clock on a Saturday night because, although Lincoln isn't a particularly lawless place, you are very vulnerable when you are trying to juggle or rope-spin.

As it turned out I needn't have worried because there was plenty of security around and the people were friendly enough. But there were times, in the early evening, when there weren't very many around and it was during one of those times, when I had thankfully decided to keep on going, that an agent happened to be walking by on the opposite pavement.

Without me realising it, he stopped to watch for a few moments and it wasn't long before I was on his books.

Chapter Fourteen

Spotty Arrives on the Scene

In November 1988, a new face joined our show. Or perhaps it wasn't so much of a face, as a six-foot tall Dalmatian dog. It wasn't a real one, of course, but a costume which had been created to tie in with the showing of Disney's 101 Dalmatians film at the Ritz Cinema in Lincoln some years before. I knew it was unlikely that my show would ever be able to feature real life performing animals, I just didn't have the expertise to handle them and they would never have fitted onto the back seat of my car, anyway.

But a person inside an animal costume could have almost endless possibilities, I reasoned. The animal was promptly christened Spotty - The Superdog, and it wasn't long before I had a simple routine for him (I say 'him' but it has on a number of occasions been a female inside the costume). The routine was based on an "educated pony" routine I had seen many times in Yelding's Circus. At my direction Spotty would count by raising and lowering a paw. He would guess the ages of various children in the audience by counting out the number with his paw, find the little boy in the audience who didn't keep his bedroom tidy or the little girl who was in love with a boy at her school or the biggest fool in the whole of the room, which always ended up being me, of course.

As a finale, Spotty would attempt to jump a little hurdle, which he always knocked down. Simple stuff, and I suspect there weren't many children in the audience who didn't suspect that Spotty wasn't a real animal. But even the adults seemed to get a lot of fun out of the routine. And if we were doing a child's birthday party, there was an opportunity for Spotty to walk round the tables of children while they were having their tea and to pose for photographs with the youngsters.

But Spotty did have his drawbacks. For one thing, the costume was very hot and I reckoned the maximum time anyone could comfortably spend inside the costume without coming out for air, was around seven minutes. The other snag was who could wear the costume?

One by one I enlisted the help of my various friends and I quickly realised that no matter who was inside the costume, Spotty very quickly took on a personality of his own. Even the quietest and most retiring of my friends would suddenly take on a new lease of life once enshrouded by the Spotty costume and although I always carefully rehearsed the routine with every newcomer, you were never quite sure exactly how things were going to work out and I suspect that made it all the more appealing to the children.

Spotty's first appearance was at a little boy's fifth birthday party on a Lincoln housing estate and right from the moment he first set a paw on stage he was a hit.

He wasn't featured at the venues where the audience was going to be predominantly adult. At places like that I was still featuring "Peter's Challenge", where members of the audience had to come up with unusual objects for me to juggle with and just as I thought I had been set just about every challenge you could imagine, someone would come up with something different.

At a church social in a village hall not far from Lincoln, I found myself having to tackle two sponges and a boot, three water-filled rubber gloves, three bottle tops, three shoes and a thimble and two spoons, with varying degrees of success.

Happily, as it was a church gathering, I wasn't confronted with various items of female underwear to juggle with on this occasion.

By now the show was increasingly going out under the name of Circus Funtime, and in March 1989, in a bid to get the name better known, I offered a free performance of the show for a charity auction run by BBC Radio Lincolnshire.

To be honest there wasn't an enormous response but in the end the offer of a free show for a child's birthday party, was sold for £15, and I reckoned we had had more than that amount in free publicity from the programme, so I was quite happy about it.

A few weeks later, I was lucky enough to have some more television work, this time as an extra in Central Television's production of Boon. The series was very successful in its day, and starred Michael Elphick, David Daker, Bridget Forsyth and Tim Healey.

It wasn't so much of a walk-on part, as a sit-still-and-pretend-to-eat part. It was filmed over a period of ten-and-a-half-hours at the Commodore Suite in Nottingham and I had to sit at a night club table, along with lots of other people, watching Tim Healey doing a stand-up comedy routine.

It wasn't a particularly arduous task and I considered I had been quite well paid for all my efforts - although there was a lot of standing around to do during the day. The episode was broadcast in October to around ten million viewers and, if you knew exactly where to look, you would have spotted me on screen for all of fourteen seconds.

Despite all my best efforts, I was finding I was getting more and more requests to work outdoors with my juggling act and I have always found this particularly difficult to do. Even on a day when the sun is actually shining, an unexpected gust of wind can play havoc with the props and when it's raining then life becomes almost impossible.

So when I was booked to appear at the old Lincoln Carholme racecourse a few weeks later for the Lincoln Carnival, I wasn't very happy when it looked as if it was going to turn out to be one of the wettest early June Saturdays on record.

Fortunately, by the time I was due to work at around five o'clock, the rain had eased off but most of the people had got soaked through during the afternoon and had wandered off home long before I arrived. So I found myself standing out in the rain, trying to entertain an audience of around twenty, huddled under the shelter of a grandstand.

Talk about "flaming June" it was more like "flaming December!"

Children sometimes ask me if Pedro the Clown has a birthday? Well, I suppose he does and that day has got to be Sunday, July 2, 1989. My partner and I, along with our old friend magician Paul Kane, had been booked for ten Sunday afternoon shows at the Embassy Centre in Skegness.

Because of Paul's other commitments, he was unable to do every one of the Sundays with us and on the days that he couldn't be there his place was taken by another very good friend of ours, magician Ron Bradford, whom I had known since our days at

North Hykeham Amateur Dramatic Society.

We had originally planned for the show to be called Circus Funtime but for some reason that I never really did understand, the bills described it as Circus Showtime, which I suppose was near enough.

The show was due to start at two o'clock every Sunday afternoon and you don't have to think very hard to realise that you are on hiding to nothing with a show that starts at two o'clock on a Sunday afternoon at the seaside. If the weather's good, then you can't expect to drag the people in off the beach and if the weather's bad then probably the day visitors haven't come to the seaside anyway.

So we were never destined to make any huge impact on a theatre which was capable of holding more than twelve hundred people. But we gave it our best shot.

A couple of hours before the curtain was due to go up, we would arrive and set the stage. Then at around one o'clock, my partner would set off in a loudspeaker van, kindly provided by East Lindsey District Council which owned the Embassy Centre, either she - or on one memorable occasion - the driver, would be wearing the Spotty costume.

Meanwhile I was outside the doors to the theatre, juggling away trying to encourage people to come in and see the show. Sometimes it worked. Sometimes it didn't.

There were only three of us in the show but with costume changes the aim was to give the impression there were several more, so El Petanos would open the show with rope-spinning. I would then nip off to change, leaving Paul to do his first magic spot. Then I would return as Pedro to do a couple of comedy routines, finishing up with Spotty. After the interval,

Paul opened the second half with his magic and we finished off as El Petanos again with the juggling, ghost entrée and disco ribbons.

Including the interval the show lasted for one hour and forty minutes and by the time the audience had got up from their seats, we were standing in the foyer to wish them goodbye and to thank them for coming.

After the first week, someone suggested that Pedro ought to get at least one custard pie in his face and it was duly written into the script.

As the weeks went on the council had some cut-price leaflets printed and we would arrive in the town by mid-morning and distribute them around the streets in costume. It wasn't entirely a waste of time because audiences varied in number of three hundred to a mere forty and I can tell you that just forty people in a theatre built for twelve hundred, is hard going - especially when it comes to comedy.

Skegness wasn't our only seaside resort that summer. There was the occasional booking at a club in Cleethorpes and our first visit to a lovely little caravan and chalet park at a place called Tunstall. Now, I pride myself on knowing every seaside resort in Britain. It's not something I ever set out to do and it's not something I boast about but it's a knowledge I have built up over the years mainly through my work. But when our agent told us we were going to Tunstall, I admit that I had to take a long, hard look at my atlas of the British Isles, and eventually I found it tucked away on the Yorkshire coast not far from Withernsea.

It was a long way to travel after a day at the office and it was after midnight before I arrived home again but I fell in love with the place straight away and was always glad whenever I was booked back there again.

By the beginning of October we would normally

have expected to be working back inland again with the end of the holiday season. But not this time. We found ourselves booked for Sunderland illuminations. It was a long journey by any stretch of the imagination but we were booked in for the first Saturday night in October and by staying overnight with my niece in Bishop Auckland, it meant I was spared the late night drive all the way back home.

Now, to be absolutely honest it had never occurred to me that Sunderland was anything more than a large town on the coast, so straight away I must owe a huge apology to the Sunderland Tourist Board. Because it's no mean seaside resort either.

But as I drove through rain-lashed streets in the fading light, there didn't seem to be a soul about and the seafront was in darkness. Though once night fell, what a transformation. I love Blackpool Illuminations (and I am firmly convinced that it should be made compulsory for everybody in Britain to visit them at least once a year) but it seemed to be that Sunderland's ran them a very close second.

They went on for miles and I was to appear at a venue called the Seaburn Centre, close to an amusement park. It wasn't an ideal venue. Very big and I worked on some sort of temporary stage surrounded by bouncy castles. And bearing in mind the thousands of people who were walking up and down outside, admiring the lights, I don't think I counted more than sixty people in the audience.

This show, by the way, was something of a landmark for me because I used, for the first time, my own microphone and speaker, which I had bought just a few weeks earlier from a magician in Skegness. I had paid the princely sum of £75 for it and it's been a jolly good investment, because at the time of writing

I am still using it.

The speaker may be looking its age a little now and it weighs a ton-and-a-half (all right, I am exaggerating a little there) but it sounds as good as ever and many a time I have been grateful for it. The Seaburn Centre was one of those occasions, because without it I am sure that very few people in the hall would have heard a word I was saying.

That Christmas among the venues I appeared at was Lincoln Fire Station Social Club. It was one of those occasions when, bearing in mind the venue, I had decided not to use my fire torches. But we had just got nicely into the ghost entrée when the alarm bell sounded, and all the firemen in the audience had to dash off quickly and disappeared down those famous poles and out onto the fire engines.

Saturdays in mid-December can still be very hectic and they certainly were in the late 1980s. On one day I remember doing a fifty-minute in-store promotion at a supermarket in the centre of Lincoln soon after ten in the morning. By a quarter-past two we were on stage at a working men's club near Barnsley, and just over a couple of hours later we were appearing in a factory canteen near Doncaster.

The journeys weren't incredibly long but there wasn't a lot of time to spare between them and bearing in mind that there was only one more Saturday before Christmas, the towns and roads were all choc-a-bloc. And to make matters worse, I think they were digging up a stretch of the main road between Barnsley and Doncaster as well and the traffic seemed to tail back for miles.

Somehow, I suspect possibly more by luck than good judgment, we made it, and the only untoward things that happened were getting hopelessly lost trying to find the factory canteen, and Spotty the Superdog falling off the edge of the stage at Doncaster.

To be honest it was a very small stage and luckily it wasn't too far off the ground.

The following summer I added another couple of seaside places to the list of venues I had never heard of. During the first weekend in May, we were booked for a holiday park at a place called Skipsea on the Yorkshire coast. As I remember, it's one of those villages that you have to go to rather than through. And although it didn't seem to boast a lot of amenities, it did have a very nice holiday park and I was booked to give a thirty-minute children's show in one room and another thirty-minute adult show, a couple of hours later, in another room.

For once it wasn't one of those occasions when there were too few people for the size of the rooms. Over the two shows, I reckon there was a total audience of more than 1,000 but the trouble was many of them were just too far away from the stage and it was a lot easier for the adults in particular, to carry on talking and drinking without realising that a show was taking place.

Patrington Haven was a different kettle of fish. We appeared in a kind of youth club building at a caravan park, on the shores of the Humber and the audience of around sixty was near enough to feel a part of it all.

Our only appearance at Mablethorpe that summer was at the Carnival Gala on the Sherwood Playing Field. Apart from doing a couple of spots on the edge of the field, there was a parade around the field at the start of the afternoon, which included one of my friends, Wayne, in the Spotty costume. Now, as I said, I reckon that seven minutes is about maximum time for anyone to spend in the Spotty costume, and this was a very hot day. By the time we completed the parade, Wayne had been in the costume for quite a considerable length of time, and we ought really to have weighed him before and after, because I am sure he shed more pounds than he earned that day.

The following week, after doing a couple of spots at a families day in a club at R.A.F. Scampton, we then went a few hundred yards down the road to the County Showground where the Lincolnshire Steam and Vintage Rally was taking place. I have always had a soft spot for a steam rally and at one time I was on the committee which ran the event.

Now, once the day time crowds have gone home, the event takes on a whole new appearance. After dark the lights go on in the old-time fair, the fairground organs strike up and many of the engines are in steam. On a warm August evening there's nothing quite like it and thousands of people, who stay overnight at caravan rallies on the ground, turn out and wander round with a glass in their hands, listening to the music and soaking up the atmosphere.

The organisers of the event are lucky in that they have the use of the large exhibition hall on the showground and that's where they hold a family disco. As a break from the dancing, they had a cabaret at around ten o'clock and that was my contribution to it all.

It was one of those events when you felt privileged to be even a small part of it all.

Chapter Fifteen

It Ended in a Riot

Some shows you remember as being very, very good, when the audience was receptive and seemed to enjoy and appreciate what you did. Others you remember as a complete and utter disaster. Fortunately the disasters tend to be few and far between but a few days after the steam rally I attempted to do, what I think is still, the most difficult show I have ever done.

It was on a big council estate which wasn't renown for its high standard of behaviour and visits from the local constabulary weren't exactly unknown. This particular time the police had got together with various sections of the community to come up with a play scheme which would run right through the summer holidays, in a bid to keep some of the youngsters off the streets.

And I think it had been working very well - until the last event of them all. It was a disco in the local community centre and this would probably have gone very well too, if it hadn't been for the fact that some of the tickets had fallen into the hands of youngsters from a rival council estate nearby. And the two did not meet - or at least if they met, they did not mingle and they did not get on.

As we arrived at the community centre and began unloading our props into the hall, I remember feeling just a little uneasy as I spotted the locals sitting out on the edge of the pavement, their feet in the road and cups of tea in their hands, obviously waiting for something to happen. But I am always the optimist and I know I have frequently gone down well in a place where the locals have the opportunity to see little in the way of live entertainment and not very much money to spare.

But you couldn't mistake the atmosphere outside the hall and inside it was even worse.

The disco started off at around half-past-six, early enough for the youngest children in the hall. But it wasn't long before you began to realise that, although there was a reasonable police presence in the hall, things weren't going well.

One little boy, who couldn't have been more than ten, mooned at my partner as she was setting out the props on the stage. A little girl of around the same age, took one look at the costume I was wearing and asked what I was going to do.

I gave her my best beaming smile and announced: "We are going to do a show."

And I was completely deflated when she countered: "What's a show?"

We did our twenty minutes on stage and then had to bundle everything off into a kitchen when something approaching a riot broke out in the main hall. Along with some of the children from the nearby estate, we were locked in the kitchen for our own protection. Blood was shed and although I don't think anyone was seriously hurt, punches were thrown and one or two people may have taken the opportunity to have settled some old scores.

But it wasn't until the hall had been cleared, that we were able to get our props out and into the car, which I was delighted (and rather surprised) to find hadn't been vandalised. Still in costume, I drove off the estate as quickly as I could and it was a long time before I went back again.

That November we were back in Sunderland again and it had to be the last weekend of the season for the illuminations, because it was the first Saturday in November. This time, we had been booked to appear in a small marquee sited on the grass verge almost on the edge of the promenade and across the road from a large fountain.

One of the locals told me that from time to time the people had been known to put washing up liquid into the fountain and watch the bubbles cascading down the street. But there weren't any bubbles around this particular night. It was so windy that I would swear the surf from the sea was breaking against the walls of the tent.

I remember we had a job finding the tent, because according to our contract it was in a park but we eventually ran it to earth at the side of the road. I can't remember whether there were any seats or whether the audience just stood around and watched but there must have been a mains electricity supply because I used my PA system and we didn't work in total darkness.

We did two shows that evening, managing to vary them slightly in case anyone was mad enough to come back for a second time and - with my partner no longer keen on doing the plate-spinning routine - I took over the act for the first time.

It's a funny thing but no matter how ill you may be feeling, once the time comes for you to get off into your car and do a show, then a miraculous cure seems to come over you. During the summer I am prone to hay fever. I know it's fashionable these days but I have a sneaking feeling that I probably invented it, because even in the days when nobody else seemed to have it, I was sneezing my head off from the last weekend in May until the third weekend in July.

Now sneezing and juggling don't go together. But I can be viewing the world through swollen eyes, sneezing every few seconds and croaking with a dry mouth, almost up to the moment I am about to set foot on stage and then it goes completely. I can do the show without a handkerchief in sight but the moment I have packed all my props away in the car and I am driving home, it will start again.

There must be a medical or a mental reason for it but I am blessed if I can think what it is. I am just very grateful for the fact that it happens.

It's the same with a bad cold or even flu. I remember one time in late January 1991. It was a Sunday and all day I had wrestled with my conscience about whether or not I was really up to doing the show. The thing is I hate to let anyone down. I knew it was a families night and there would be lots of disappointed children in the audience and there would be little or no chance of our agent finding another act at such short notice.

So in the end, perhaps against my better judgment, I did the show and hopefully no one in the audience would have realised how dreadful I was feeling during the sixty-five minutes on stage.

That May, I was booked to appear at the Prince's Quay Shopping Centre in Hull. It was the first time I had worked in the city and the first time I had appeared at a shopping mall.

I had heard horror stories from fellow performers who had worked at shopping malls, although none of the stories had been about Prince's Quay. Entertainers had recounted how youngsters had dropped things on them from the floors above and there had been a lot of aggravation.

So it was with some trepidation that I parked my car at the shopping centre and began carrying my props through onto a small stage which had been erected at the widest part of the centre. But it wasn't long before I realised it was going to be a trouble-free day. It was mid-week during term time and there were no children around. At least, if there were any, they weren't the sort of age you had to worry about, and there was a security camera turned permanently onto the stage so you had the comfort of knowing that someone, somewhere, was keeping an eye on you.

We did nine 12-minute shows throughout the day and the biggest problem was finding an audience. At lunchtime I counted as many as sixty people standing to watch but at other times the numbers were struggling to reach double figures and we never went back.

But that wasn't our only trip across the Humber that summer - and thank goodness for the Humber Bridge. It might have been dubbed a massive multi-million pound white elephant by many people but it did make getting to places like Hull and the Yorkshire coast that much easier and quicker for us to reach.

Apart from a couple of more trips to Tunstall during the summer, I also had the opportunity of appearing at the Driffield Steam and Vintage Rally. Driffield isn't as big as the Lincolnshire steam rally but the people are very nice and we had a good evening in the Showground Pavilion. Unusual for us, we didn't go on stage until half past ten so, although there were still a few children around, most of the routines were adapted for adult audiences.

I have mentioned before how difficult it is to work on a small stage where you run the risk of literally tripping over your props. Well, in the run-up to that Christmas I had one of the smallest working areas ever. The landlord of one of those good old traditional locals not far from Lincoln Cathedral, decided to hold a Christmas party for the children of his regulars and we were booked to give a fifty-minute show.

When we duly arrived on the Sunday afternoon, and carried my props into the lounge, I inquired in all innocence where we were going to work. "Over there," came the reply. "We are going to move the pool table."

And that was just about the only space we had. I don't know if you are familiar with the size of the average pool table but it's not very large. You can add a couple of feet on all the four sides and that was our working area. But somehow we managed to do a full show, although I think when it came to the Disco Ribbons Finale, we had to be very careful we didn't do anybody a mischief with the ribbons.

In comparison the Norprint Social Club in Boston a couple of weeks later was a dream. And for once getting the props into and out of the club couldn't have been easier.

Everything was on the ground floor and all I had to do was to back the car up to the stage door and unload straight out of the boot and onto the stage. Why can't all venues be like that.

When you appear at some venues, you get a sense of history and occasion. For instance, if you are beyond a certain age, you may well remember the days when the horse flat-racing season would traditionally open on the frequently-windswept Carholme at Lincoln. It was the scene of many a Lincolnshire Handicap before the course closed in the 1960s and the event was switched to Doncaster. But what is left of the old Lincoln racecourse, one of the grandstands and some other buildings, still survives as a reminder of those old days.

When I did a post-Christmas children's party in what used to be the weighing room at the old racecourse, I couldn't help thinking of all the winning jockeys who would have entered the building in triumph in those days gone by.

Sadly by that time the building was well beyond its best and bearing in mind we were still only just a few days into January, it wasn't particularly warm, which may not have been a good thing for the audience but it was fine for me. When a venue is very hot, I can come off stage at the end of a show, with my costume wringing wet. Sometimes I really do look and feel as if I have been through a car wash. But on this occasion I seem to remember feeling remarkably cool at the end of the show.

That summer I was to spend more time on the coast than ever before and the first place I went to at the beginning of April was the Primrose Valley Holiday Village at Filey. It was the opening night of the season for live entertainment and we appeared in the children's venue with a sixty-minute show. There seemed to be a lot of running around back stage at the start of the evening and new recruits among the entertainments staff were being constantly reminded of the need to smile.

Until then I had always assumed that everybody else - just like me - smiled without having to think about it. But it seems that if you are required to smile for a living, you have to be constantly reminded of the fact.

By the time we returned to Primrose Valley a couple of weeks later everybody seemed to be smiling to order.

A few days later we opened at Golden Sands Holiday Centre, Mablethorpe, again doing a lengthy children's show after a long and busy day at the office. This was one of those huge venues where it seemed to me you could comfortably have got more than six hundred children into the room and still have had some space to spare.

Unfortunately the stage was at one end of the room which meant that it was difficult to involve those youngsters standing or sitting at the back. It was perhaps one of those venues more suited to the Red Arrows than to a couple of people.

The next new seaside venue was a holiday centre close to Flamborough Head not far from Bridlington and later on in the season we added a holiday village just outside Great Yarmouth to the list of regular bookings for the summer.

To be honest, if there was ever a case of a "holiday camp too far" it was the one just outside Great Yarmouth. There was nothing wrong with the place at all. It was a well-kept, well run venue not far from the sea. The big problem was the distance from home.

In my youth Great Yarmouth was the place where many of our friends and relatives used to go for their main holiday during the summer. I had been myself as a child and you tended to measure your stay there in days or weeks rather than in minutes and hours as I was having to do in the summer of 1992.

It was a round-trip of 256 miles and to get there in time for my nine o'clock spot, I was having to leave the office at around half past three, drive along the busy road to Norwich and you would always find yourself stuck for mile after mile behind a slow-moving tractor, negotiate Norwich in those days before the ring road was completed and end up in

Great Yarmouth in time to unload and set the stage at around seven.

I would come off stage around ten in time to change, load the car up again and start the long drive back to Lincoln, generally not getting home until the early hours. I must admit that once, and only once, I came very close to falling asleep at the wheel and it was only the sound of the tyres running on the gravel at the side of the road that brought me back to reality.

Between times we were back at Tunstall again and did a second season of Sunday afternoons at the Embassy centre in Skegness. This time we had for company a couple called Miko and Dolly Daydream, who were wonderful old hands at the business. The only thing that worried me was that I couldn't help thinking that they ought to have been topping the bill, instead of us but they never complained at all.

This time I had succeeded in getting the show publicised as "Circus Funtime" and we would spend the morning handing out leaflets around the town before standing outside the main door to the theatre in a bid to attract in an audience and eventually doing the show.

It was while I was leafleting Skegness one Sunday morning that I found Ray Smith doing exactly the same thing. His Circus Galaxy had pitched its Big Top on the football ground at the edge of town for the summer and I couldn't help thinking we were both competing with one another.

But we gracefully accepted each other's leaflets and went on our way. A couple of weeks into the run we were to have a guest star. Keith Harris and Orville were to top the bill on one Sunday. They were in town to switch on the illuminations and I think part of the deal must have been that they did a show at the

Embassy as well.

I had been a fan of Keith's for years and it was a great thrill working with him and to discover that he was every bit as much a nice fella off stage as he was on. The only thing was that when he was standing or sitting anywhere near Orville back stage, I fell into the trap of talking to Orville rather than to Keith, although it was generally Keith who was talking back.

It wasn't just a case of having celebrities on stage either. One Sunday afternoon I was really scared and a little bit embarrassed when I spotted the legendary Jacko, one of Britain's top clowns, sitting in the audience. By that time, Jacko had retired to Skegness, after a period of ill health and he could never resist the opportunity of seeing a circus of any sort.

So it was very much a case of the tables were turned as the clown, who I had watched so many times in some of the nation's biggest circuses, was watching me trying to entertain him and our meagre audience. As soon as I spotted him, I did take the liberty of halting the show, introducing him to the rest of the audience and asking him to take a bow. I felt that was the least I could do.

More than a decade later, just before his death, I was to meet Jacko again when we were both among the audience at the Embassy Centre, watching the great Chinese State Circus.

Apart from our regular trips to and from the coast that summer, there was one slightly different sort of show inland. There was a charity cricket match at the Trent Bridge ground in Nottingham, where the stars of television's Emmerdale (or Emmerdale Farm as it may well have been called in those days), were playing a local side.

I was booked to do some walk-round

entertainment during the afternoon and couldn't resist the opportunity of including one of my favourite tricks where I juggle with a cricket bat and a couple of balls. I may well have never succeeded in playing cricket for England but at least I had the opportunity to use my schoolboy bat on the field where so many Test Matches have been played over the years.

The autumn found us busy in and around Lincoln, and one of the places we appeared at was the Blenkin Hall in Lincoln. The hall was a pretty big barn of a place but it was special because it was just a few stones throws away from where my father was buried. The hall is no more. It was demolished a few years later but among the audience on this occasion at a church harvest supper, was my old headmaster from thirty two years before, Harry Lister.

I was delighted when he agreed to come up onto the stage to take part in an audience participation spot, where he and his wife were required to try to do a few juggling tricks. And I was reminded of an end-of-term prank, when I had pinned a make-shift circus poster to the door of the staffroom with the names of various members of the teaching staff superimposed over the names of real circus artistes.

Chapter Sixteen

A Taste of Australia

When you think of the number of engagements artistes tend to do over the years, it is only to be expected that occasionally there will be some sort of mix-up. So I suppose I have been very lucky in that it hasn't happened to me very often. But a few days before Christmas 1992, I was booked through an agent to appear at a children's party in a pub not far from the Meadowhall Shopping Centre in Sheffield.

We arrived and set up on the tiny stage and were all set to start when another entertainer turned up, and we found we had both been booked for the event, when clearly there wasn't the time or the money available for us both to work.

It seemed that between my booking being made, the landlord had moved on to another pub, and the new landlord, who didn't know about the arrangement, had booked someone else.

Happily we were able to sort it out without any difficulty or embarrassment. The local entertainer took one look at the amount of stuff we had set out on stage, and realised we had done a round trip of something like a hundred miles to be there and he bowed gracefully out.

A charity show a couple of weeks into January 1993, took us to the Bishop Grosseteste College Theatre in Lincoln for the first time and it gave us the opportunity of rubbing shoulders with Glyn Owen, Mary Millar, David Griffin and Helen Atkins, who were appearing in panto in Lincoln at the time and hot-footed it up to the college theatre after the curtain had come down on their own show.

A couple of days later we took part in another charity event, which has got to be unique in Britain. The city is proud of its links with Australia, and on a visit down under, a city Mayor had seen for himself the kind of celebrations that go on for Australia Day.

The local councillors, officials and celebrities roll up their sleeves to serve a traditional Australian breakfast (which, to be honest, isn't all that different from a traditional English breakfast) to the masses, and the whole thing raises money for good causes.

And he reasoned, if such a thing does so well in Australia, why couldn't it work back in Lincoln as well? Given that Australia Day falls in the middle of an Australian summer but in the middle of an English winter, the Lincoln council decided to give it a try.

The previous year they had held an Australian Day Breakfast at The Lawn Visitor Centre in the historic heart of the city and the event had been a tremendous success. In fact, it had been so successful that they had almost run out of food.

There was no question that the breakfast would become an annual event but the council felt something had to be done to keep the lengthy queues amused while they were waiting to get into the hall. So they wanted Pedro to juggle and generally help to keep the children happy in one of the long corridors, while they were waiting for seats.

It was one of the earliest starts Pedro had ever made, appearing outside at the flag-raising ceremony at eight o'clock (it was hardly daylight) and then spending the next four hours hard at work in the corridor. But what an amazing day it was. In the 21st century the breakfast is still running and although I have by now appeared there more years than not, I still haven't lost my enthusiasm for it all.

January in Lincoln just wouldn't seem the same without it and it's a wonder the idea hasn't spread to other British towns and cities as well.

We did yet another charity show that May. Didn't we ever get paid for anything we did that year? And this one was a wonderful one-off event.

It was the 50th anniversary of the legendary Dambusters Raid by 617 Squadron on Germany, and to mark the occasion two hundred and forty special children were to get a round-Britain flight on the City of Lincoln jumbo jet, starting and finishing at the squadron's home at R.A.F. Scampton.

Before and after the flight the very excited children and their parents were accommodated in one of the large hangars and once again Pedro was needed to help keep everyone entertained before and after the flight.

At this time I had never flown. I had never really wanted to, preferring to go on holiday by cross-Channel ferry and driving to my destination. But I couldn't help feeling just a little bit envious as I watched the children entering the aircraft.

As it turned out, it was perhaps as well that I wasn't invited to join them on the flight because the aircraft was flying at an unusually-low altitude and at a slower-than-usual speed and there was quite a bit of turbulence. Even some experienced flyers admitted afterwards that they were far from well on the trip and it could have been enough to put me off flying for the rest of my life.

There are some shows you wish you had been paid for and others that you feel a little bit embarrassed because you were. The show we did in a little hotel at Filey a few weeks later certainly fell into the second category but because it was done through an agent we felt we had little alternative but to accept the money.

A little girl who lived in the town, had just come back home after a second heart operation, and friends and neighbours had done a whip-round to lay on a party for her. We did our very best to help make the party a success but I couldn't help feeling a little bit guilty at the end when we were paid.

It also marked the introduction of a new juggling prop to the show. Some time earlier I had been impressed when I saw a juggler using three large knives in his routine. Well, I call them knives but they were more like swords. So I decided it was time I got hold of a set of them myself. I quickly found they are as easy to handle as indian clubs and because they are fairly heavy, you can work them outdoors even in quite a strong wind.

And they do look impressive as well, especially when you bang them together and you get quite a loud "clang."

That summer, we were recreating "Circus Funtime" on the compact stage of the Grange Hotel and Country Club at Chapel St. Leonards, just north of Skegness. We were there for seven Sundays but unlike the previous season at Skegness these shows weren't going to start until eight o'clock, which meant we had a better chance of attracting a large audience - or so we thought, until the first week when there were only thirty people in the room.

After that once the schools had broken up for the summer, the place was filled most evenings, although I had misgivings about the final show at the end of the season, because it was during the village carnival week and we were up against the rival attraction of a free firework display. But I needn't have worried. The concert room was packed and we were able to time the show so that the interval coincided with the firework display, so everyone was able to go outside to watch and then come back for the rest of the evening.

That summer I met Don Lusby, who apart from being a big circus fan, ran a dance school in Scunthorpe and was also a prominent member of the Humberside and Lincolnshire Music Hall Society. They were an amateur/semi-professional group of talented entertainers, who raised money for good causes by doing a number of shows. Would I be interested in taking part in one of them, he asked.

Although Don is no longer with us, he falls into the category of "those who have been a great help to me in my show business efforts along the way", and the show I did for him at the Polish Social Centre in Scunthorpe was the first of a number at different venues. But more of that later.

That Christmas we were appearing in Birmingham for the first time, thanks to an agent who seemed to have a vast and impressive list of venues at his disposal. The first booking was at a factory social club in Smethwick. Now I knew absolutely nothing about Smethwick, expect that it had once figured in some sort of nasty riot, so I was hoping it wouldn't turn into the unpleasant scenes we had found ourselves caught up a couple of years earlier.

But I needn't have worried because the people couldn't have been nicer and it was the first of a number of venues we played in and around Birmingham.

The next day we were back in Lincoln with a

children's party at the cellar bar at the Constitutional Club in Silver Street. If ever there was a venue that was difficult for loading and unloading, it was this one. And for that reason and for that reason alone, I wasn't at all sorry to see the "closed" sign go up on the door some years later.

It was impossible to park alongside the pavement outside and the nearest car park was some distance away. On a weekday or Saturday you wouldn't have stood a chance of parking there but luckily our show was on a Sunday afternoon and it was in those days before the shops were allowed to open on Sundays. So having parked, we were then faced with carrying the props and costumes through the car park, along the pavement, into the building, down a flight of stairs and into the bar.

And, just to make things worse, it was snowing.

Our first booking in 1994 was back in Birmingham, this time a children's party at a social club in Sheldon Heath. Now, all the social clubs I had ever appeared at anywhere in or around Lincoln were generally smallish buildings where the stage, if it existed at all, was a modest affair - sometimes no more than a few boxes bolted together.

But the one at Sheldon Heath had to be seen to be believed. By social club standards it was enormous and at least comparable in size to the stage of the Theatre Royal in Lincoln. You felt good from the moment you stepped out onto it and I hope the performance reflected how we felt.

I was able to do a couple more shows for Dan Lusby soon afterwards, first at his dance school presentations in Scunthorpe and then for his Music Hall Society at the Four Seasons, a night spot just down the road from where I lived. I was originally booked to do a twenty-minute spot with the juggling, plate-spinning and rope-spinning but when I arrived, there was panic.

The compere hadn't turned up and it didn't look as if he was going to make it. Nobody had an evening suit with them so, as I lived the closest, I was despatched homewards to get my evening suit and to compere the show - in addition to doing my own spot. It was the first time I had ever been asked to compere a show, other than my own and the biggest problem was that most of the acts I was introducing had some bewildering names which it was almost impossible to pronounce correctly.

But I don't think I could have offended too many of them, because I was destined to do more shows with the group in the months ahead.

Over the years we have done birthday parties for a host of individual children and just occasionally for twins. But in February 1994 we had a first when we did a birthday party for triplets. It was held at a club at R.A.F. Wittering, alongside the A1 just south of Stamford. Hardly had we finished there, than we were back up the A1 to Lincoln for another charity show at the Bishop Grosseteste College, this time with John Challis of Only Fools and Horses fame.

Working to such tight schedules it would be impossible if we weren't to leave various props behind from time to time and that's what we did that day at Wittering. Luckily it wasn't an essential piece of equipment, just a microphone stand but it was a very long way to go back to collect it some days later.

A couple of weeks later, a showman friend of mine, William Wood, who I have mentioned previously, invited me to clown at Stamford Mid-Lent Fair in the south of Lincolnshire. Once again it was a long way away from home but there was no way I was ever going to say no to this one. I love fairs and Stamford street fair is one of the best I have ever attended anywhere.

As a teenager there was even one very memorable occasion when I had ridden there on my Lambretta in March and stayed overnight at the Crown Hotel, so I could be right in the middle of the fair and enjoy it to the full without having to ride back the same night.

By coincidence William even arranged for me to change into my clown gear in one of the rooms at the Crown Hotel in 1994. It may even have been the very same room that I had stayed in during my last visit to the fair.

The rides and stalls are scattered throughout the town centre and car parks with a number of streets closed to traffic for the week. William controlled a section of the fair in Bath Row and he was anxious to create something of a carnival atmosphere, so he had arranged a veteran steam engine to be present, he had put bunting across the street and booked a handful of entertainers, including myself.

I didn't know it at the time but it was to be the first of my annual visits to Stamford and they have continued right up to the present time. In some towns and cities working in the street can be a bit of a nightmare because you never quite know when you are going to come across trouble. But Stamford is different. In all the years I have been going there, I can't remember ever having any sort of bother, whether it's on a Saturday afternoon, an early weekday evening or after nine o'clock on a Saturday night.

You can even put your bag or box of props down

on the pavement, walk away and talk to some people and come back a few minutes later and everything is exactly where you left it. And you can't say that about many places.

By this time Pedro was beginning to take over. I seemed to be getting more and more bookings for the clown than I was as El Petanos and in a way this made things easier for me. Whenever anyone inquired about El Petanos, I then had to go into a lengthy explanation about what I was, how I was dressed and the sort of acts I did. Were they suitable for children or adults, or what? But as Pedro the Clown I didn't have that problem.

You just mention the word "clown" and everybody knows exactly what you are and what you do.

Unfortunately there are still some people who will always be afraid of clowns and I can never understand why. Fair enough, if you are a very young child and you spot a strangely-dressed person in the street, with a bright red curly wig, red nose and odd boots, you might well be forgiven for wanting to hot foot it down the road. But it's surprising just how often I have come across teenagers and even fully grown men and women, who have got a thing about clowns and can't bear to stand near one.

Sometimes, particularly when I am working in the street, a gang of lads or girls will come over to me and say "Our mate's scared stiff of clowns, will you go over and frighten him (or her)."

Of course I never do but if I get the opportunity I go and talk to them, explain exactly who and what I am and I can generally end up shaking hands with them and hopefully their problem is cured. I am afraid that my stock answer to any young lady who tells me she is afraid of clowns, is that I am afraid of pretty girls, so that makes us even.

Shortly after my Stamford debut, I was present at the start of a little bit of history in Lincoln. The city was at long last going to get a university and to launch the whole fundraising scheme the pavilion at the County Showground was hired for an exhibition, when Richard Branson was among the special guests.

Not surprisingly the organisers didn't want Pedro (I suppose he might have given the wrong sort of image) but they wanted a juggler for the evening and I appeared in what must have been one of the first Lincoln University Tee-shirts with sporty track suit bottoms.

It was an enjoyable evening but I can't actually remember Mr. Branson coming over to take a closer look at what I was doing.

I have always loved taking part in carnival processions, whether it's through a tiny village or in the heart of a big city and I think in terms of distance, the Mayor's Carnival Procession at Lincoln took a lot of beating.

We would generally start off at the West Common and walk the couple of miles to the South Common, taking something like an hour to do it. Now, the big problem you had in organising a carnival procession in Lincoln (as I quickly discovered because I was on the organising committee) was the city's famous level crossings. These days there is only one level crossing and it goes right across the High Street on the approach to the Central Station. But there was a long time when there was a second level crossing just a couple of hundred yards down the High Street.

No matter what time you planned the procession to start and finish you were bound to catch at least one of the level crossing barriers closed to road traffic. Many is the time when the band leading the parade has got to within a few feet of the crossing and the barriers have come down, bringing everything to a halt.

Worse still, there have been times when half of the procession has successfully got over the crossing, then the barriers have come down bringing the rest of the decorated floats and entertainers to a halt.

I think it is partly for this reason and partly because it became increasingly difficult to persuade haulage firms to part with their lorries and drivers free of charge that the parade was finally abandoned. But I have some very happy memories of them.

Having made my fairground debut, it wasn't long before Pedro was invited by Yorkshire showman Roger Tuby to appear on the opening day of Doncaster's 800th Charter Fair, which was located on a couple of town centre car parks.

Roger asked if I could find another clown to accompany me, so I pressed one of my Echo colleagues into service and we ended up getting changed and making up in the back of a lorry. You couldn't help thinking it must have been a bit bewildering when a couple of reasonably-smartly dressed men disappeared into the back of a fairground lorry and re-appeared a few minutes later as two very strange-looking individuals. But it's surprising what you can get away with in the name of entertainment.

Chapter Seventeen

We Nearly Did a Runner

That summer went by in a blur of corporate events, holiday camps and parties. Sometimes we would be working in the loading bay of a printing works; the next weekend you might be in a country pub in rural Yorkshire and the next you could find yourself in the front room of a private house.

It wasn't long before the Christmas parties arrived and we were back in Birmingham once again. Until now we had always been booked to appear in what I had considered must have been the top social clubs in and around the city and in some of the nicest areas. But my opinion was revised very quickly just a week short of Christmas Day.

We arrived at this club on a Sunday afternoon and I must admit our faces fell immediately. The building looked like a fortress. There were no windows. They had either been boarded up or bricked over. There was wire to stop people from climbing onto the flat roof and a sea of broken glass in the car park. And some of that broken glass looked like the remains of vehicle windscreens.

It was sometime before I could bring myself to switch off my car engine and make my way into the club and I didn't feel any more at ease when a man, who I believe was on the committee, indicated a heap of broken glass outside the back door and told me: "We had a disco here last night. We didn't like him, so we smashed his van up."

And it was no comfort when he added: "You've got two hundred kids this afternoon. I wish you luck."

As if that wasn't enough, the stage was one of those incredibly small ones with no height and no depth and I was very tempted to load everything back into my car and bid everyone a "Merry Christmas" and drive off into the gathering gloom. It wasn't so much courage that kept me there or the thought that I didn't want to let down an agent, who until then had been very kind to us but the stark realisation that if I did try to make a break for it I would be lucky to get out of the car park.

So I went ahead and did the show; got paid in full and was promptly rebooked for the following year. Sometimes there is a danger in reading too much into a first impression.

By the start of 1995, a new name was hitting the headlines all over Britain. It was an American group of male dancers called The Chippendales, who were filling theatres all over the country with screaming women. Their claim to fame was that they looked athletic young men, several of them had long hair and as they danced around the stage they managed to take most of their clothes off.

I had a return booking coming up for the Humberside and Lincolnshire Music Hall Society at Scunthorpe and I badly needed a new adult routine for the show. So I came up with something that I called "Almost a Chippendale".

Now you have got to bear in mind that I was fast approaching my 50th birthday, so I was probably twice the age of the average Chippendale. My hair was still pretty long and curly, although there was a bald patch at the back that I was getting a little self-conscious about and there was a little more weight around my tummy region than I would have preferred.

I was working solo, so I felt I could take a few liberties with my costume without embarrassing an assistant. In the best Chippendale tradition I decided to wear a black bow tie, no shirt, a very brief pair of black underwear - which meant I was reasonably decent at the front but there wasn't a lot around the back - and, oh yes, a pair of black boots.

I daren't tell anyone I knew what I was going to do. I had never before appeared on stage wearing such little clothing and I wasn't satisfied in my own mind if I really ought to do it. So to help me decide, I shot a video of me doing the rope-spinning and plate-spinning routine in my own front room and night after night for several weeks, I would play it over trying to decide in my own mind if I was really doing the right thing or just making a complete and utter fool of myself.

I even videoed the routine with me wearing rather more clothes but I decided if the whole thing was to work I had to wear the briefest of briefs.

But on the night of the show I still took another costume with me just in case courage failed me at the last minute.

The venue was a large pub on the western side of Scunthorpe. Although there was a small stage at one end of the room, the show was being performed on the dance floor immediately in front of it and the audience sat around tables on three sides, cabaret style. An organist was providing the music and there were about eighty people in the room - most of them female and most of them elderly.

I did my first spot, juggling in a red tight-fitting cat suit with a white satin shirt and for the second spot I decided on the brief costume and thought:

"Let's go for it."

I have never had such a reception as I had that night. The audience and everyone in the show fell about laughing. I didn't exactly have the ladies swooning at my feet but at least it must have given them something to talk about on their way home and I think it was generally agreed among the members of the society that next time I did one of their shows I should give a repeat performance of my routine.

Easter was spent at Skegness, where the venue this time was the Suncastle Family Room. By any standards it was going to be a long night. We were the only act on and in addition to doing two spots - one as El Petanos and the other as Pedro - we had to do a session of party dances afterwards.

The get-in was formidable. I had to park in a garden at the side of the pavement in Grand Parade and then carry everything down a path, through a courtyard and down the length of the family room to the stage at the far end. The stage was so small most of the show had to be performed on the floor and perhaps, worst of all, there was no dressing room.

So we improvised in the way that only a desperate clown can. Somewhere at the back of the room, we found a plastic awning, which at one time would have graced the top of a hot dog stall. By propping it up against a wall there was just room - and only just room - for one person at a time to change behind it. Take a step too far, one side or the other, and there was a very real danger of a large section of the audience seeing a bit more of Pedro than was intended.

To get over the problem of having to make up in such a confined space, my partner hit on the idea of making me up in public so everyone could see how it was done. It was a stroke of genius really because it filled in another five minutes on stage as well.

It was the first of several weeks we spent at the Suncastle and if ever anyone had decided throw the hot dog awning away, I really don't know what the alternative would have been.

That summer the nation was marking the 50th anniversary of V.E. Day and one of the biggest events in Lincoln was the Mayor's Carnival Parade, which was re-scheduled to coincide with the anniversary and was given a suitable theme. Despite being held several weeks earlier than usual, the parade was blessed with the warmest and sunniest weather we had ever enjoyed and we must have walked slower than usual or there must have been more trains around, because we took an extra twenty minutes for the parade to reach its destination.

When you are juggling in a parade, you have to bear in mind that you don't always notice what's going on around you. The vintage car immediately behind you might be getting uncomfortably close or the decorated float in front might be getting too far away. And there's very little opportunity to glance down at your feet to see what you might be stepping in.

That year, the parade was blessed with a number of horses which naturally did what horses do and unfortunately at the busiest spot in High Street, I stepped right into a freshly-deposited lump of horse droppings.

I am not quite sure what the horse had been eating but I know my boots were a very strange colour by the time we finished the parade.

Shortly afterwards I found myself working at a very unusual venue and in front of a very special group of youngsters. Russia was still getting over the

Chernobyl disaster and a group in Lincoln had forged a link with the stricken community and were welcoming a group of twenty Soviet children to the city for a holiday. None of the children appeared to speak English and the organisers wanted to show them what Britain was really like. So they entertained them to a traditional fish and chip lunch and I did a thirty-minute clown show round the back of the chip shop for them afterwards.

My biggest disappointment of the year came the first weekend in September. Through my work at the Lincolnshire Echo, I had heard that the National Ambulance and Emergency Services Show was about to be held in Lincolnshire for the first time and the venue was the County Showground.

With ambulances and their crews coming from all over the country, it sounded like just the sort of thing I ought to be involved with. I was able to tip one or two of my fairground friends off about it. They duly set up a small fair on the site and I was booked to give a series of thirty-minute clown shows inside the exhibition hall throughout the day.

There ought to have been thousands of people on the site looking at the emergency crews in action, marvelling at the various types of ambulances on show and letting their hair down at the fair. But there weren't. I don't think I have ever seen so few people at any event on the County Showground. It was almost as if someone had forgotten to unlock the gates to let them in.

You couldn't blame the weather. You couldn't blame the advance publicity. I don't know what the answer was. But I know that my best audience of the day was only forty strong. Everybody must have lost a lot of money and for one of the few times in my life

I readily agreed to hand back some of my appearance money.

That autumn William Wood was launching a new fair on the Recreation Ground in Stamford. It was to be the town's first autumn fair for something like thirty years, and the first time a Stamford fair had been held on grass for ages, as the much bigger Mid-Lent Fair was always held in the streets.

William asked if we could clown for him during and after the official opening ceremony. We were due to appear at my eldest grand-daughter's fifth birthday party in Portsmouth the previous evening, so we were able to call in at Stamford on the way back to Lincoln without too much trouble.

After changing behind a fairground organ, we spent a pleasant hour-and-a-half around the fair, and once again it was to be the start of a very long and successful run of appearances at the autumn fair.

The time was when if I was working outdoors it would generally be during the spring, summer or early autumn months. But by now, the pattern of the British pre-Christmas activities was changing. Spurred on by the very successful Lincoln Christmas Market, which had been set up in the 1980s and eventually copied by just about every self-respecting town, city and village in the country, Barton-upon-Humber had decided to hold a Christmas festival of its own in 1995.

My showman friend, John Armitage, who lives in the town, was providing the fairground on a car park in the High Street and there were trade and charity stalls right through the town centre.

I was booked to work in the street, almost straight across the road from the fair, non-stop from 6.15p.m. to 8.45p.m. Luckily it was a very mild, dry and windless night for the first day in December and I got away with it. The council, which organised the event, didn't want me to clown on this occasion. They had other clowns booked to work in other parts of the town centre, so I did my show in the black trousers I had driven up in, plus a lot of woollies and a fancy waistcoat on top.

It was just as well really because, as far as I could see, there was nowhere for me to get changed, so for once my car had to be the dressing room.

But it was a terrific evening and the start of what was to be a very long and happy association with the town. If Stamford is my special place in the south of Lincolnshire, then Barton-upon-Humber is my special place in the north.

For a town of its size, it's amazing just how much goes on there and over the years I seem to have been involved in quite a lot of the activities.

I had my first chance to appear at the now legendary Lincoln Christmas Market the following week but on this occasion I was indoors, working in arguably the oldest pub in the city, the Lion and Snake in historic Bailgate. Once again it was for a party for a group of children from Chernobyl. There was hardly any room to work. The place was heaving and it was never really designed for live entertainment anyway but it was an evening to remember.

After a town centre promotion and a couple of parties in Sleaford, our next booking took us back to Birmingham and I must admit I had had nightmares about this particular run of shows. In fact, I think my concern had even brought on an attack of shingles a few days earlier. We were doing three full hour-long shows in three different venues on the Saturday and another one on the Sunday, staying overnight at a

Travel Lodge to avoid the long drive back.

My biggest worry was that the three Saturday shows were in different parts of the city and there didn't seem to be a lot of time between them. If our agent hadn't had the foresight to give me a copy of the Birmingham A to Z well in advance, I think I would really have had problems.

We arrived at the first venue in Erdington well in time for the eleven o'clock show, managed to do the show, load everything back into the car and drive over to Tyseley for the second show at 2.30p.m. Then there was just enough time to dash over to Washwood Heath, where we were appearing at a children's party for Leyland Daf Vans.

The first thing that struck us was the size of the Washwood venue. There were three hundred children in the hall and if you had opened the big doors down the bottom, I am sure The Red Arrows could have flown in. The building was enormous.

Everything was going well until mid-way through the show, when I lit my fire torches and all hell, I am sorry, a dreadful commotion broke out. My fire torches had activated the smoke sensor and the works fire brigade turned out. I glanced to the side of the stage to find a man in a dark blue uniform and yellow helmet looking back at me. Luckily the children seemed to take it all in good part. There was no evacuation of the building and, because it was Christmas, nothing more was said about it.

My first booking of 1996 was back in Birmingham, this time at a factory social club on the south side of the city.

"I hope you're better than the act we had last night," was the greeting. "It was the Barron Knights, and they only did two-and-a-half hours."

I closed my eyes and crossed my fingers, hoping that my own seventy-minute programme would be quite long enough, particularly as I had only been booked for an hour.

After an overnight stay in Birmingham, we did a children's party at Acock's Green the following day and it was one of those occasions when you are booked to do an hour but for one reason or another, you suddenly find yourself having to do twice as long. Whether another act or disco hadn't turned up, I can't remember but for the extra sixty minutes we had to do a selection of party dances and some joke-telling to keep the youngsters amused. Luckily our extra efforts were reflected in the money we were paid.

It's a very important lesson for a children's entertainer. Always carry a tape of party dances with you. You never know just when it is going to come in useful.

I was back in the streets of Sleaford a couple of weeks later on a very cold and cloudy January day, as one of a number of entertainers booked to help attract shoppers to the town. I was being paid by either the town council or the chamber of trade, so I wasn't busking and didn't have to rely on shoppers to toss coins into a suitcase at the side of me.

But one shopper thrust a pound coin into my hand as she went on her way and I was so surprised that I must admit I kept it for a long time as a souvenir of the day.

Chapter Eighteen

Almost a Chippendale Again!

In March, between visits to Stamford Mid-Lent Fair, I was booked for a return show with the Humberside and Lincolnshire Music Hall Society, which by this time had changed its name to the Northern Music Hall. The venue was once again the Berkeley Hotel - scene of my previous year's exploits in my "Almost a Chippendale" routine.

Although I was a year older, I still felt confident enough to give a repeat performance of my previous year's act, although this time, for the first of my two spots, I added a new routine which was to become very important to me.

For years I had been wanting to do the Tower of Tumblers act. You must have seen it. You have two small tables, some distance apart, and there is a supply of plastic tumblers and metal trays under both of them. You gradually build up a tower made up of a tray with four tumblers, with another tray with four tumblers on top of that and another tray with four tumblers on top of that and so on until the tower is complete.

The only thing that had prevented me from doing the act before was the lack of height at most of the venues I worked. To do the routine properly you might need as many as twenty or thirty trays but I have managed to get away with ten or eleven and, although the top of the tower has been scraping the ceiling at a number of venues, the whole thing has never yet ended in a disaster of my own making.

The Tower of Tumblers was well received but it was nothing compared to the reception I got when I returned in the second half of the show, dressed in little more than my black briefs. I must admit I was getting quite blasé about appearing in public wearing just my underwear and it was almost certainly the nearest I shall ever get to being a male stripper.

The Lincoln Mayor's Carnival Procession that year took place on my birthday and the occasion was duly announced to the watching crowd by my old friend the Lincoln Town Crier, Terry Stubbings and later over the loudspeaker system. Although it was a hot and sunny day, the watching crowds were smaller than usual because of the counter attraction of the Euro 96 soccer competition on the television. It was noticeable that most of the onlookers were women shoppers, who had come out of the house to escape yet another afternoon of televised soccer.

A few weeks later I was back at Barton-upon-Humber again, this time for the carnival in the lovely Baysgarth Park. It was basically a two-hour walk round, greeting visitors at the gate with my juggling and spending as much time in the fairground as possible.

In August Lincoln was celebrating a special date in the city's history. It was 150 years since the first train had steamed its way into the city and I was on a committee set up to organise events for the big day.

A highlight was to be a Rail Fair on the car park of the Central Station and I had persuaded showman Robert Hill to set up his Snake Slide and kiddies train ride on one corner of the car park to provide a landmark for the event. There was a steam traction engine from the local Museum of Lincolnshire Life and some suitably railway-themed stalls but the crowds were lacking. And it didn't help that what was to have been the main attraction, a steam-hauled passenger train, had to be cancelled at short notice.

But I spent a pleasant few hours each day juggling my way around the car park and meeting lots of old friends.

In October I was booked for another appearance with the Northern Music Hall and this time the group had moved out of the Berkeley Hotel into the much bigger Baths Hall. I think the hall got its name because there used to be a swimming pool there. In fact, the pool may still have been in position, hidden away somewhere beneath the floor.

A decade or two earlier some of the biggest names in the pop world had appeared there and with four hundred people in the audience, it gave me another opportunity to present my "Almost a Chippendale" routine, along with the juggling, rope-spinning, plate-spinning and Tower of Tumblers. Now whenever I go back to a place on a regular basis, I try to vary the show as far as possible but it isn't very easy because I don't have that big a range of material, which can be used for adult-only audiences.

It's not like a singer, where he or she can perform different songs or a comedian who can come up with some new gags. A speciality act is far more restricted. However on this occasion I had managed to come up with something just a little bit different.

Some weeks earlier I had gone to the cinema and seen a man in an advert juggling three cans of lager or beer. What he was doing was fairly basic stuff but it was the props he was using that made it so memorable.

As a children's entertainer, the idea of tossing cans

of booze around in front of impressionable young faces might have been frowned upon. So I decided to use something children would identify with and I did what I called my "Cascading Coke Cans". I have kept them in my show ever since and yes, they no longer contain "the real thing". If they did, I am afraid they would have exploded many years ago, so I drained them and filled them with paper to make them a suitable weight.

I have never managed to do anything particularly clever with them but because they are such a novel prop, it's usually enough to capture the children's imagination. To avoid any problem with exploding cans, I usually preface the trick with the time-honoured warning: "Don't try this at home." Just occasionally I will add the words: "Wait until you get to someone else's home."

My return visit to Barton-upon-Humber Christmas Festival a few weeks later had become two days instead of one and it was wonderful to see the streets thronged with people, not to mention a large number of civic leaders from towns in the surrounding area.

After taking part in the Mid-Lent and Autumn fun fairs, I was delighted to go back to Stamford at the beginning of December for the civic switch-on of the Christmas lights. Apart from walking up and down the High Street juggling bean bags, I had the opportunity to work in William Wood's can-can stall with a marvellous character called Mick.

Mick was a "gaff lad" or "fairground worker" in his late teens but what he lacked in years he certainly made up for in confidence and really had the gift of the gab. He was a dab hand when it came to encourage people to try their hand at knocking the tin cans from the shelf. And his cries of "Would you like a pooh girls," were legend (I must point out here that the prizes on offer were large cuddly Winnie the Pooh bears).

It was to be the first of many occasions that Pedro would be seen working behind one of William's stalls.

Wouldn't it be great if all your ideas were successful. If everything you touched turned to gold. Well they don't, as I found out just a few days later.

Ever since it had started I had visited Lincoln Christmas Market every year and looked at the vast crowds that filled the streets between the avenues of stalls. Estimates of the size of the crowds put the number of visitors at around a quarter-of-a-million over the four days and I thought surely there could be something in this for Pedro.

So I spoke nicely to the headmaster of Westgate School, which was right in the heart of the market. They were already doing quite well raising funds by selling refreshments to the market visitors in the school hall. As an old boy of Westgate - in fact it had been in the school playground where I had first taught myself to juggle - I thought this had to be the place for me to try to earn my fortune at the market.

I was allowed to use one of the classrooms for a series of thirty-minute circus shows on the market's two busiest days on the understanding that I wouldn't use my fire torches and that I would make a donation to school funds. I thought I could hardly go wrong.

I had some posters printed advertising shows at 5p.m., 6.30p.m. and 8p.m. on the Saturday and at 12.30p.m., 2p.m., 3.30p.m., 5p.m. and 6.30p.m. on the Sunday, and displayed them around the local shops. I fastened a large billboard to the school fence announcing "Pedro the Clown - here today" and even stood at the gate in costume trying to entice people in.

The price of admission was very reasonable, although I can't remember what it was now and I needed only a very small percentage of the people who past the gate to step inside, to attract reasonable audiences.

But what I hadn't reckoned on was how the crowd was made up. When you stood and looked at them, there weren't a lot of children to be seen. It was mainly mums out on a coach trip or mums and dads who had decided to leave their youngsters at home to avoid the crowds.

Fewer than forty people were at the three shows on the Saturday evening. I never had more than fourteen at any of the shows on the Sunday, and the first and the last ones of the day had to be cancelled because no one at all turned up. In the end, I made a £16 donation to the funds of my old school, paid out my expenses and made a profit of £17 for my two days work.

A year or so later a full travelling circus pitched its Big Top on the nearby grounds of The Lawn Visitor Centre for the Christmas Market and presented a series of short shows which were far superior to anything I had to offer. But I suspect they met with a similar response, because they never went back again.

I bow to no one in my admiration for the Christmas Market but when it comes to trying to entice the visitors inside - either into a classroom or a Big Top - it just doesn't seem to work.

I optimistically billed 1997 as my "30th anniversary tour," even having tee-shirts made with the message on and including the words on all my publicity for the year. But at the start I never realised just what a momentous year it was to be in my life and in my semi-professional career as Pedro the Clown.

I made my Derbyshire debut a couple of days into the New Year when I appeared at a hotel in South Normanton for the children of showmen, who spend the winter on a nearby estate. The event marked the tenth anniversary of the opening of the Selston Winter Quarters and, apart from having to drive through a heavy snowstorm most of the way there and a thick fog most of the way back, it wasn't a particularly difficult evening.

But shortly afterwards I found myself in a domestic crisis with the prospect of having to cope on and off stage by myself.

Daughter Karen, who by that time had moved back to Lincolnshire with her family, knew most of the routines and assisted whenever and wherever she could but with a young family to bring up she was never going to have that much spare time available.

It wasn't always practical to rely on an outsider to work as my assistant, so I came to realise there was only one thing for it. If Pedro the Clown was to continue, he would have to work as a solo act for the foreseeable future at least. The routines that could be worked solo would remain. Others, which required at least two people to make them work, would have to be mothballed.

Fortunately, although there was still work available on the coast, I was getting an increasing number of inquiries for walk-rounds or promotions and these I felt confident enough to do on my own.

One of the first was at Scunthorpe Easter Fair for Yorkshire showman Sheldon Dowse. The evening before the fair was due to open to the public he was giving the freedom of the rides to something like two hundred special children and he asked me to go along.

It was a wonderful occasion, helped by some mild and still weather and I think everyone got a kick out of seeing the youngsters enjoying themselves on the rides and it was the start of a tradition which continues to this day.

Although I didn't know it at the time, it was to be the last fair ever held on the Station Road Playing Field before the site was turned over to housing. I still have a bit of a lump in my throat every time I drive by the housing estate and remember the fairs and circuses they used to hold there. If the present-day residents are ever haunted by the spooky sounds of children's laughter or of ghostly dodgem cars going bump in the night, it serves them right.

It was around this time I made my first appearance at Elsham Hall near Brigg and although I couldn't have guessed it at the time, the venue was to have a lasting influence on my life in time to come.

My first show there, on what would have been my wedding anniversary, involved doing a couple of spots during a cabaret and dinner in the Barn Theatre, an impressive venue with a courtyard on one side and open fields on the other. It was Don Lusby who first introduced me to the venue but I never really had the opportunity to thank him because he became ill and died not long afterwards.

I am sure the entertainment scene in and around Scunthorpe is a lot poorer for his passing.

I was back at Elsham again for a couple of days over the Spring Bank Holiday as Pedro the Clown doing two or three different shows a day.

Just when it looked as if the amount of summer work was beginning to dry up, it was once again

William Wood who came to the rescue. I think he must have decided I needed something to keep myself occupied at weekends, while I got used to my new domestic arrangements, and he set me to work in his hoopla stall, sometimes with Mick and sometimes on my own, at the side of Brayford Pool for the newly-revamped Lincoln Water Festival.

Unfortunately the event lived up to its name and it wasn't just the water in Brayford Pool. Throughout the weekend it rained and it rained and it rained. It may have been the third week in June but you wouldn't have guessed it. The carnival parade up High Street was a wash-out. Apart from a few people huddled in the shelter of the shop doorways, there was no one around to watch the parade make its way through the city centre.

The rain ruined most of the floats and I ended up travelling inside a vintage bus, which let in so much rain that at the end of the journey I was probably just as wet as I would have been if I had walked the whole way.

It was also thanks to William that I found myself back in Derbyshire a couple of weekends later. On the Saturday I was at Bakewell Carnival Fair, held for what turned out to be the final time on the Cattle Market Car Park, before moving further out of town. I spent five very happy hours in costume, taking money on the can can stall, the mini-waltzer and the bouncy castle as well. As the night wore on I left and returned out of costume to help dismantle the stall at the end of the fair. Although I am no stranger to travelling fairs, I couldn't get over how quickly the rides and stalls could be dismantled once the crowds had gone home. In almost the time it took for me to walk round to the other side of the stall, serve a couple of customers and walk back again, the children's cups and saucers ride nearby had been folded up, hitched to the back of a car and taken away. Despite my best intentions, I think the stall I was manning must have been the last to pack up - not because we were taking money long after everybody else had stopped but because it took me so long trying to understand where everything went and how it came apart.

That night I slept in the bunk in the cab of a lorry, before we set off the next day to the grounds of a big house in a village not far from Derby. The owner was giving a party for his children and while most would have settled for a bouncy castle, he had booked an impressive Formula ride, which is a number of eye-catching little cars and trucks going round and round a track, and a giant slide which was built onto the back of an articulated lorry.

And all this for just twenty children.

Pedro gave a mini show outdoors and thoroughly enjoyed himself on the rides, just as much as the children.

Yorkshire Television's Calendar Roadshow came to the grounds of Lincoln Castle towards the end of July and I was invited to juggle among the crowd and was later thrilled to see myself on screen for all of thirty seconds.

With Karen's assistance I was able to do a number of shows at one of my favourite pubs in Ingoldmells that summer. I used to spend a lot of time in the village when I had a static caravan there and on the occasions when I called in anywhere for a drink it was more likely than not to be The Bell.

It had a sort of balcony outside where you could sit and watch the traffic and holidaymakers going by, so I was quite pleased when my agent booked me in for some evenings in the family room. Unfortunately the get-in was a big problem. You had to unload in a public car park nearby, carry all the props up the stairs onto the promenade, through an open seated area and the length of the family room to the working area.

I would swear that on the first time I was there they didn't have a stage and I worked on the floor. But on subsequent visits they had created a tiny stage with an even tinier dressing room behind it. Also, on at least one occasion, they didn't switch off the coin-operated machines which lined the walls, so you found yourself competing against the dreaded Space Invaders and Pac Man with all their loud and musical accompaniment. But by and large it was a good place to work.

Towards the end of the summer, I was back again at Elsham, this time at a medieval banquet. This was to become something of a regular booking for me, and I even had a special costume made for the venue. It was also a rare treat to be working with other entertainers as in those days, when many venues were watching their budgets, you would quite often be the only act on the bill.

But at Elsham I enjoyed the company of a very accomplished jester, a unicyclist, fire-eaters and magicians. Although it was hard work for something like three-and-a-half hours, everybody was usually in good spirits and the man in charge, Robert Elwes, always ensured there was a meal for you before you went home at the end of the night. It might sound a common enough courtesy but it's surprising how many venues don't think to make even a glass of water available for the artiste, who has probably driven many miles to get there.

Chapter Nineteen

A Day We Will Never Forget

For a long time I had been looking forward to the final weekend in August, when I was to be heavily involved in a charity gala, followed by a cabaret, buffet and dance at The Lawn in Lincoln. The organiser, Kate Clarricoats, had really put her heart and soul into the event and, although it was going to be a long day, everybody hoped it would raise a lot of money for the Lincolnshire Air Ambulance.

What we didn't know was that it would be a day we would never forget.

We were due to open the gates at ten o'clock on Sunday, August 31 and, when I turned on the radio at home a couple of hours earlier, the news was breaking that Princess Diana had been killed in a car crash in Paris.

The nation was stunned. Everybody was glued to their televisions and radios watching as the story unfolded. Nobody wanted to go out and enjoy themselves and yet all the arrangements had been made for the gala, acts had been booked, caterers had been arranged and far from raising money for charity, the event would have cost the organiser quite a bit of cash if everything was called off.

It was a decision which had to be taken quickly and it was something without precedent. Whatever the organisers did, they knew they were almost certain to be criticised for it. So in the end the day went ahead as planned.

At ten o'clock I was standing at the gates to The Lawn clad in make-up, wig and tartan suit, not knowing whether to laugh or keep a dignified silence. And quite a few people were arriving not having heard the news of the tragedy before they left home.

"Why is the cathedral bell tolling?" asked one family. "Has someone died?"

How do you answer a question like that when you are standing there dressed as a clown?

A highlight of the gala was to have been the Supermarket Trolley Grand Prix - an event I had first launched on an unsuspecting public some years earlier at the Lincolnshire Steam Spectacular. I was due to compere the race in the arena, with the teams trotting round to the theme from Chariots of Fire, while I identified the individuals over the public address system and related some interesting facts about them.

We then held a number of heats with teams from local supermarkets pushing their trolleys around an obstacle course. Normally that event can go so well with the crowds getting behind the teams from their favourite store to cheer them on but on that miserable Sunday nobody had the heart for it and I have never tried to revive the event again.

The evening cabaret went little better. Just about a hundred people turned up and although the entertainers tried to carry on as though nothing had happened - because we were conscious people had paid quite a lot of money to be there - far from being a day we would like to remember, it turned into a day we would rather forget.

I couldn't complain too much about the working conditions at a party I did the following October, because I wasn't in a social club, pub or church hall.

The event took place in my own front room. My grand-daughter Leigh-Ann was seven years old and for convenience we had her party for just ten children at my house. With the assistance of the birthday girl's mum, Karen, we put on quite a creditable little show but it's the only time I have ever "appeared" in my own house and it was a very weird experience.

Shortly before Christmas I was back at Elsham Hall for a series of medieval banquets and in between entertaining the diners everybody was asked to pop into the adjoining Granary Restaurant where there was a small private party taking place. During a break, I went over to do my Tower of Tumblers, rope-spinning and juggling routines, before going back into the main hall for the plate-spinning. It made for a busy evening, so I wasn't entirely happy to find one or two of the guests in the restaurant appeared to be the worse for drink.

I had just completed my Tower of Tumblers and made my usual announcement: "And now comes the most difficult bit - taking it all down again!" when a man at one of the tables piped up: "No it doesn't" and threw a bread roll straight at the tower. Of course, the whole lot came crashing down with metal trays and plastic tumblers everywhere. Luckily no one was hit and there was no serious damage done. Somehow I managed to keep a smile on my face and make some kind of joke out of it, although I was far from happy - particularly as I had been doing that part of the evening as a favour and wasn't getting paid for it.

Of all the times I have done that routine for rooms full of unruly children I had never had any trouble at all. But do the same thing in front of a room full of men and women in evening dress and that happens.

At around this time, I think Elsham had a

wonderful assortment of entertainers working there. The banquets were presided over by George who was the Barron and he acted and looked the part perfectly. John was the very camp jester with an ability to reduce even the most straight-laced lady to fits of laughter. There was Tim who juggled and rode a unicycle, often at great personal risk because sometimes the floor was slippery, Peter who played the lute very successfully and Rodney and Linda from the world of circus.

Rodney owned Circus Markus and, apart from being a real nice man and fun to work with, his main part of the programme was a knife-throwing routine. With his daughter Linda assisting him, he would persuade members of the audience to come out onto the floor and stand in front of the knife board while he threw knives all round them.

Nothing would ever have induced me to do it, although I had every faith in Rodney's ability. But conditions at Elsham weren't ideal for that sort of act, because if you didn't keep an eye open, you found you had members of the audience wandering between Rodney and the knife board, on their way to or from the toilet.

Although I generally tend to get changed into my costume once I reach a venue, there are times when you can't, particularly if it's an outdoor event and there may be nowhere you can strip off out of public gaze. So there are times when I have to drive some fairly lengthy distances dressed as Pedro the Clown. And you get some very interesting reactions from passersby and other road users - although, as far as I am aware, I have never yet been responsible for causing a serious road accident. One thing I have to do on these trips is to make sure I have enough fuel in my car to get me to and from my destination, because I am sure if I went into a petrol station dressed like a clown, someone would assume I was going to rob the place.

On those trips I also generally try to avoid driving through busy town or city centres, where I know I am likely to be held up at traffic lights or level crossings. But sometimes you can't avoid it. While most children, if they happen to spot you at the wheel of your car, will laugh and wave, the reaction from teenagers and fully-grown adults can be very varied.

I was on a narrow country lane heading for a gala one sunny morning and pulled over to allow an oncoming vehicle to pass. The driver, a man not of tender years, must have spotted the clown's face through the windscreen as he approached, so he drew up alongside, stopped, wound down his window and we spent a pleasant few minutes discussing where I was heading for and what I was going to do.

Outside a barracks at Kirton-in-Lindsey one afternoon there was a small group of soldiers waiting by the main gate and I must admit I had expected some cat-calls or rude gestures as I drove by. But in my rear view mirror I spotted nothing but waves and smiles.

During the first half of 1998 I was spending more and more time at Elsham. If it wasn't medieval banquets it was a series of half-hour children's shows over the bank holiday weekends, or themed-weddings and if it wasn't that it was a Vaudeville show. And it was over the Spring Bank Holiday when one particular booking was to change my life.

I was doing three shows a day in the Barn Theatre when I met Lynn, who was working her way through university as a mature student and had a part-time job in charge of the catering at the theatre. We got talking during quiet moments and soon realised we had feelings for one another, although it must have been some time before she first saw my face when it wasn't entirely covered by greasepaint and make-up.

Fortunately, right from the start, Lynn took a keen interest in the entertainment side of my activities and often used to accompany me to my bookings. But I don't think she was best pleased the day I was doing a walk-round at Barton Carnival that summer, accompanied by Lynn, and one of the youngsters described her as "the clown's mother" particularly as Lynn is considerably younger than I am.

On August bank Holiday Monday I reached a landmark in my life, with my 1,000th gig. It was at John Proctor's fair on the Holywell Cross Roundabout in the centre of Chesterfield. It was a glorious hot and sunny day and I spent three hours as Pedro juggling my way around the rides and stalls, meeting some lovely people who were all in the holiday spirit and enjoying every minute of it. At times when the crowd thinned out, I would move nearer to one of the main entrances in the hope of attracting more people into the fair.

I couldn't help thinking that this was what it was really all about. And the famous crooked spire of Chesterfield, just around the corner from the fair, seemed to make the day even more special. Before I left the fairground, I mentioned to John that it had been a special day for me because of the 1,000th gig and I thought no more of it. But John had decided to do something about it and a few weeks later, a certificate arrived, signed by the Mayor of Chesterfield, recording the fact that my 1,000th show had been in the town.

It was a wonderful surprise and a certificate that I still treasure.

Autumn brought a return to Elsham; a fire station gala at Lincoln where one of the main attractions was parachuting teddy bears dropped from the platform of a fire engine with an hydraulic lifting tower; a brand new fair run by Keith Carroll at Sleaford and fairs at marvellous Matlock (where the site on the Bridge Car Park seemed to be almost permanently under threat of being lost to redevelopment) and Stamford. Sometimes I would be accompanying the local mayor as he or she performed the opening ceremony from one of the rides, other times I would be walking round juggling, chatting to the families and trying to attract passersbys in.

Although I had actually performed my 1,000th show at Chesterfield a few weeks earlier, a variety show at the old Four Seasons in Dunholme was widely billed as the 1,000th. The main reason was that the Dunholme show had been arranged for several months in advance and based on the bookings I had at the time, I made a calculated guess that I would reach my landmark by mid-October. As it turned out, I was a few weeks out but by then the advertising had been done and there was no going back.

The show had been expertly arranged by Lincoln entertainer Mac Baker, who got a group of performers together to present an old-style variety show to help Kate Clarricoats raise money for the Air Ambulance. Apart from doing our own individual spots, Mac had devised the show so that we would all get together on stage for a number of comedy routines. In one of them I was required to dress up as a young lady and perform the much-loved (or much-hated, depending on how you looked at it) song called Sisters, which had been made famous a long time earlier by The Beverley Sisters.

Using three large mock-up television sets, we also did a "changing channels" routine where I was the presenter of a gardening programme.

Later on in the show I played the part of an over-the-top 60s television reporter describing the scene as Elvis flew in to one of our local air bases to give a show, with Mac in the role as Elvis.

In our plate-spinning routine, which came fairly near to the start of the show, Lynn assisted me on stage for the first time. But the moment I will never forget, was when it all went horribly wrong. We had carefully rehearsed it for weeks. Someone had very kindly made me a pair of trousers which would fall apart at a touch - or at least a fairly hefty tug.

The idea was that I would go out on stage and start to juggle with my fire torches and Lynn and one of the other young ladies would tug at my trousers which would fall apart, leaving me in a very brief pair of briefs. Unfortunately, the trousers decided they would fall apart of their own accord sooner than they ought to have done, leaving me to cover my modesty with a copy of the Lincolnshire Echo, which happened to be at the side of the stage.

I have got the whole thing on video, so if there ever comes a time when I find myself feeling too big for my boots, I just put the tape on and I am quickly reminded just how vulnerable we all are on stage.

Some time after that the Four Seasons closed its doors for the last time - absolutely nothing to do with that night. The cabaret suite was later destroyed by fire (again, absolutely nothing to do with me) and now the remains of the building stand awaiting an uncertain future. What a great pity, because I had some memorable evenings there as both a journalist, interviewing some of the big name cabaret acts which appeared there and entertaining at children's parties and charity shows.

It was shortly afterwards that Pedro underwent a major change in face make-up. To be honest I hadn't been entirely satisfied with the original look for some time. My face was almost entirely white and, apart from a red nose which I have always painted on top of my real one, there wasn't a lot of colour. But Lynn gave me some useful tips on how to add colour and more features to my face and when I next appeared at the civic opening of Belper Fair in the town centre later in the month, Pedro looked rather different and I hope less like the phantom of the opera.

The run-up to Christmas brought a return to Barton-upon-Humber Festival and a charity show at the town's New Queen's Club the following lunchtime, where Lynn appeared as Spotty the Superdog for the first time.

I was fairly heavily committed with pre-Christmas shows, when the unexpected happened. I was leaving the office in the dark one early evening and got my feet entangled in a looped piece of binding tape which someone had left on the ground. I pitched forward onto the concrete, dislocated a couple of fingers in my left hand, hit my forehead and ended up in hospital.

My biggest worry was the damage to my hand, because once the fingers had been put back into place, I was very limited to what I could do with them in the near future and I didn't know what permanent damage to expect.

Clearly juggling was out of the question for the time being, so I quickly had to cancel the most immediate medieval banquets and children's parties. For a time I convinced myself that I would probably never be able to juggle again and I must have been like a bear with a sore head for days, because it really brought it home just how important juggling was to me.

There had been one pre-Christmas booking I had been reluctant to cancel because it was a circus workshop at a village school not far from Lincoln. Apart from talking to groups of pupils and giving them some basic tips on juggling, Lynn and I were also giving a couple of 30-minute shows to round the day off. Clearly using heavy props like the tennis rackets, hammers and knives was out of the question and I restricted my juggling to bean bags and three Coke cans.

Psychologically the day had given me something of a tonic because it did prove that I was still capable of doing a show. All I had to do now was to concentrate on getting the full use back in my left hand. To be on the safe side I cancelled the rest of the Medieval banquets at Elsham and concentrated on getting myself as fit as possible for a booking at the Legionnaires Club in Sleaford on Boxing Night.

The juggling act was still very much reduced but to more than compensate for this we now had Lynn's fire-eating which she presented under the name of "The Dragon Lady".

Much to the surprise of our neighbours, she had been rehearsing in our back garden at home. Her father had made her a "wheel of fire" with four torches which revolved around a mouth-piece and looked very spectacular, especially in a darkened room. She could also extinguish the flames in her mouth, run the burning torches up and down her arms, and blow a very impressive flame. Bearing in mind she was self taught and all in a matter of weeks,

I was very impressed and more importantly the audience loved it as well.

Fortunately the post-Christmas period was quiet so I had a full month to try to get my left hand working properly again. By the Great Australia Day Breakfast at The Lawn at the end of January I was juggling bean bags, rings, clubs and Coke cans again and just a few days afterwards, I was doing the fire torches once more.

My first attempt at producing and compering a complete show, came at the end of February. The Mayor of North Hykeham, Reg Poole, who I had got to know pretty well during his year of office, asked if I would put on a show for his civic charity.

I was given a fairly free hand at assembling the acts, so in a moment of weakness I accepted the challenge. And the most difficult part had to be finding the acts who were available, who I thought would entertain an audience which would include around 40 mayors and council chairmen and who would be prepared to work for nothing.

We had opted for a Sunday night at the end of February, which I gauged would be the time of year when performers might have a few gaps in their diaries. We booked the hall of the Robert Pattinson School at North Hykeham and sold around 220 tickets. R.A.F. Waddington Voluntary Pipe Band started the evening off by marching through the hall in traditional manner and assembling in front of the stage as I brought the Mayor onto the stage for his official welcome.

My old friend Dee Dee Lee then presented the first of her singing and dancing routines and Lynn and I closed the first half with our Tower of Tumblers and plate spinning.

I opened the second half and introduced North Hykeham Schools Jazz Band, which was a tremendous hit. As compere, I then had to cover what seemed to be a lengthy period as the band's chairs and equipment was removed and the stage cleared for Dee Dee Lee's second spot, so I resorted to telling a couple of the stories which I usually included in my talks.

Later I did my juggling and Lynn did her fire-eating and I was a bit alarmed to see tiny pools of burning paraffin landing on the floor of the stage but they didn't seem to be doing any damage and just added to the general effect. The Pipe Band rounded off the show, which finished with the inevitable raffle and speeches and at the end of the evening I was surprised to find the whole thing had gone on for close on three hours.

I hope the time went as quickly for the audience as it had for me. The show raised almost £1,900 for charity and one of the things that most people seemed to comment on was the fact that every time I appeared on stage to introduce the next act I was wearing something different.

Sometimes I would be in evening dress. Other times a coloured shirt and black trousers or a lounge suit. But I have got to confess it wasn't an original idea. I had got it from the compere of a show I had once seen in Blackpool and I thought it well worth copying. Also, it does give you something to do between acts and I am one of those people who need to feel busy on and back stage, otherwise I tend to get a bit nervous.

By now we were ready to include Lynn's "The Dragon Lady" fire-eating routine into the show on a regular basis but we needed some good publicity pictures, and who better than my old friend Mike Maloney. Then chief photographer at the Mirror Group and the winner of more awards than I could keep track of, Mike willingly agreed to do a photo shoot in the grounds of the Lincolnshire University on the edge of Brayford Pool.

What anyone who happened to be driving or walking past at the time thought about it I don't know but on a very cold Saturday at the beginning of March, she spent close on ten minutes blowing flames, while Mike did his usual first class job of taking perhaps the most spectacular pictures Lynn has ever had.

A couple of weeks later Lynn made her first appearance as Choo Choo the Clown with me in the streets of Stamford for the town's Mid-Lent Fair and on the Saturday night I clocked up my 1,000th juggling spot.

Easter brought an entirely new venue for us. One of the large amusement arcades in Ingoldmells had just expanded by adding an upstairs family suite which they had decided to call BJ's Big Top Showbar. They wanted a circus-style cabaret act for the children and I was thrilled when we were asked to do the very first show in the new venue. For three nights over the Easter weekend we did a 30-minute show, and apart from the get-in (which involved going up and down a lengthy flight of metal stairs many times) it was an easy venue to work. The only trouble was people would wander in at any time, so we might start with about 20 people in the audience but by the time you finished there could have been anything up to 200 in the room. It was very tempting to keep stopping to update the newcomers on what they had missed but there was really no alternative but to carry on because we were on a reasonably tight schedule as there were other acts coming on later in the evening.

We were back there again for a couple of nights over the May Day Bank Holiday and again for a couple of nights over the Spring Bank Holiday weekend.

It's always a bit special to be invited back to one of your old schools to present a cabaret or clowning show. By this time I had already been back to Eastgate, Mount Street, Westgate and Rosemary Secondary Modern schools. The only one which was still outstanding was my old grammar school in Wragby Road, Lincoln. And I was eventually able to appear there in May, thanks to the National Operatic and Dramatic Amateur Association, which was celebrating its centenary with an event at the school.

I had proposed a toast to the school at the Old Pupils Association annual dinner the previous evening and the following afternoon I was back there again with Lynn doing a 25-minute show which included the Tower of Tumblers, juggling, plate-spinning and Lynn's fire eating.

Apart from appearing at Ingoldmells during the Spring Bank Holiday weekend, we were also working at Carrington Steam Rally on a site between Boston and Horncastle.

It's the longest-running steam rally in Lincolnshire, and it's always a pleasure to visit whether as Pedro the Clown or with my notebook and camera on behalf of The World's Fair.

In 1999, Lynn and I were appearing on a stage which was in fact the trailer of an articulated lorry. You are protected from the elements on three sides but you are fairly high off the ground so it's not particularly easy getting children up from the audience to take part in some of the routines. I think we were sharing the facilities with a number of other acts including a female dance group, so changing accommodation was very limited.

It was to be the start of a number of very happy visits to Carrington in the role of Pedro.

Working outdoors does pose problems with the weather and not just with anything that is likely to fall upon you in the shape of drizzle, rain or hail but with the effect the weather has had on the ground you are walking on. When Sherman Wynn booked us for his fair at Market Harborough in what ought to have been flaming June, we found that instead of our light, brightly coloured clown boots, we would have been better off wearing Wellingtons.

We were there for two days including the Sunday afternoon, which was the first time the town's fairs had been allowed to open on the Sabbath. As I remember the field in Farndon Road was very close to a river or a sizeable stream and on the days of our visit it wasn't all that easy to see where the river ended and the field began. It was very, very muddy and we spent most of our time stepping and jumping from planks and boards spread across the ground.

The weather during our visits wasn't bad but the damage had been done a few days earlier and the result was that there weren't a lot of people around.

At the time Sherman seemed to be plagued with the weather (or perhaps it was us) because when he booked us to appear in Ashbourne a couple of weekends later, we never even succeeded in changing into our costumes. It was raining so heavily that we all decided it was hardly worth getting out of the car and if the fair opened at all that day, it shut very soon afterwards.

We didn't have any problems with the weather the following week, when Lynn and I were booked for a school gala in a village just south of Lincoln. We took part in a parade through the village streets first and did a walk-round on the gala field before our own 30-minute spot on the stage. And it was the stage which gave us our biggest worry. It was composed almost entirely of straw bales, with mats or planks of wood on top.

It was a very hot and sunny day and I had visions of Lynn or I setting the stage alight, when it came to the fire-eating and fire juggling but all went well. Just one dropped torch and I suppose it would have been a fairly instant barbeque.

Sometimes as Pedro the Clown, I get to do the sort of things I would never do otherwise. During that summer, for instance, William Wood asked if I would run his children's roundabout for an afternoon, alongside Brayford Pool for the Lincoln Water Carnival. Even with my very limited technical knowledge, it didn't take a lot of understanding. I think there was a green button to press to start it off and a red button to bring it all to a halt again.

You had to nip round and take the money from the mums and dads, before starting the ride and keeping a watchful eye open to make sure none of the riders looked like harming themselves. Then at the end of a couple of minutes, you would bring everything to a stop and hopefully the children would be safely reunited with their parents.

The trick was to try to make sure that the ride stopped in the same position as it had been when it started, then the parents could just reach out and lift their children off. But occasionally some parents would confuse you by changing their positions once the ride had begun to move.

As a clown I could get away with a lot the usual operators couldn't. For instance, you could wave and call out "Hello" to the children as the ride went round and shout out things like "The more you smile the faster the ride goes." And if there happened to be a couple of cycles among the toys on the ride, then you could assure the children who happened to be on them that the faster they pedalled the faster the ride went round.

It was all good, harmless fun and six hours went by very quickly, particularly as it was one of those occasions when the Water Carnival was blessed with some fine weather.

As I have said before, some of the indoor venues we work, have very tiny stages. But there was one village we went to on the East Coast, where for the life of me I couldn't see anywhere to work at all. It was a fairly new pub very close to the sea, and the owners wanted some live entertainment to compete with all the other pubs and clubs in the area. There was no stage, in fact there wasn't even a clear area of floor anywhere near big enough for what we did and we were booked for several dates right through the summer.

In the end I worked out the trick was to get in early and re-arrange the chairs and tables in such a way that we had just about enough room to work in an area in front of one of the exits. We even managed to do a limited version of Lynn's fire-eating act and I was able to juggle with my fire torches but I can't help thinking that, if we tried to do a similar thing today, we would fall foul of half-a-dozen regulations or laws.

Later in the month we were back at Barton-upon-

Humber Carnival and the glorious summer weather continued. Apart from presenting our children's show a number of times each day in a large marquee, I compered an item in the grand ring where scores of children and adults did a tug-o-war competition with a steam traction engine.

It's always good for a laugh, because no matter how hard the people pull on the rope, you know they haven't got the ghost of a chance of moving the engine. Very often the driver will play along with the crowd and just when they think the engine's beaten, he will do a steam engine's equivalent to putting his foot on the accelerator, and steam off.

Again with today's insurance problems, many organisers would probably think twice about including an event like this in their arena programmes these days but it used to be a cheap way of entertaining a crowd for up to 15 minutes or so.

Shortly afterwards I had one of those rare opportunities to appear on television. Central were taking their six o'clock magazine programme out into the towns and cities they served and Lincoln was to be one of them. For each programme they were having a local journalist or someone similar to act as a guide to viewers around the various spots of interest. I was invited to do it in the dual role of Peter Brown (journalist) and Pedro the Clown. That meant in some scenes I was in costume and in others I was wearing a suit.

Everything took place on the Monday. At lunchtime, I did a 30-second promo interview on the castle battlements with the cathedral in the background and this went out live to promote Thursday's screening of the main show. Then Lynn and I spent a couple of hours in Castle Hill and in the castle grounds, being interviewed and doing the fire and juggling routines.

Later, out of costume, I had to film sequences around the city centre and after all that I think it added up to something like five minutes on screen. It wasn't a life-changing experience and it didn't lead to a lucrative television career but at least Lynn and I enjoyed our brief spell in the spotlight.

As I have said before, one of the biggest problems working out of doors is finding somewhere to make-up and change into costume. My appearance at a medieval market and fair in Chesterfield Market Place that week posed a particular problem. Because, as far as I could work out, there wasn't anywhere remotely near the site, where I could park. The problem was made worse by the fact that Lynn and I were travelling in separate cars for some reason.

We lost each other in Chesterfield's congested streets and had the devil's own job finding one another again. John Proctor, who had booked us, had suggested we should change in the ghost train but we were so late getting there, by the time we did arrive the market was in full swing and there was such a queue waiting for the ghost train, you couldn't really expect the showman in charge to shut the ride for half-an-hour or so, while I got changed.

In the end a show lady came to my rescue and I changed in her booth. When we went back for the August Bank Holiday fair the following month, things were so much easier. We parked on the car park across the road from the fair and changed in one of the showmen's caravans.

I have never yet appeared in the tropics as Pedro the Clown but I could have been forgiven for thinking I wasn't that far from the equator with an outdoor booking we had at a pub on the edge of Newark that September. It wasn't just hot. The sun was blazing down and we did a 75-minute show in the full force of it. At the end of it I felt as if I had just played a 90-minute soccer final at Wembley and could have rung the sweat out of my costume.

When it comes to nice places and nice people, Woodhall Spa takes a lot of beating. It was once a place I never seemed to appear at but in more recent times I have been there at least once a year and it's a great place to be. We appeared at the Woodhall Spa Festival on the last Saturday in September. It was probably too late in the year for an event like that but the weather was pretty good and, apart from the odd shower, we didn't get too wet.

We did a walk-round in the village streets before going off to the picturesque Jubilee Park where a scout camp was taking place. After we did an impromptu show there for the youngsters, someone asked if Lynn could light their camp fire by blowing one of her flames. It wasn't easy, because the flames tend to rise and the fire was, of course, down at ground level. I can't quite remember how she did it but she did and everyone seemed to be impressed.

Lynn and I had enjoyed a very busy summer along the coast but even in early November we hadn't quite said goodbye to the seaside for another winter. Showman John Armitage was staging a firework fair on the promenade at Cleethorpes and on the opening night he invited us along for an hour or so. Now, even on a mid-summer's day it can be pretty nippy on the seafront at Cleethorpes and by the beginning of November it is getting very cold. So armed with two or three lots of clothing, we changed in John's seafront amusement arcade and walked down to the promenade where we were photographed with the Mayor and on some of the rides.

There weren't a lot of people around and to add a bit more colour, John gave me a huge bundle of helium-filled balloons and asked me to hand them out to the children. I think it might have worked out to two balloons for every child but sadly very few of the youngsters got any.

An unexpected gust of wind snatched most of them out of my hand and they were last seen sailing off into the night sky in the direction of Spurn Head. I had visions of reading in the paper the next night how the coast guard had been inundated with calls about an unidentified flying object in the sky. But the cloud of gas-filled balloons must have escaped everyone's notice.

By now the thoughts of many people were concentrating on the coming millennium celebrations, and for once it seemed as if New Year was going to outshine Christmas. We had a good December and were quietly optimistic about being in demand on New Year's Eve but in the end we had the night off.

There had been all sorts of stories in the papers and on television about how anyone who worked that night was guaranteed to make a fortune. But although we had inquiries for the night, the only firm request I can remember was from someone who wanted us for a private party in a big house somewhere and reading between the lines all we would have been were baby-sitters for the children of the guests.

So in the end we decided to have the night off.

Chapter Twenty

The New Millennium

Britain's first fairground season of the new millennium started at King's Lynn with the civic opening of the Mart, which took place on Saturday, February 12. The town centre was packed and Lynn and I proudly walked in procession with the civic leaders into the Tuesday Market Place for the opening ceremony in front of a set of galloping horses.

Donald Gray, of the Eastern Counties Section of the Showmen's Guild, even arranged a hotel room for us to relax in during the day and after the opening ceremony I was back on the streets of King's Lynn in costume that evening, as people arrived for a firework display.

The weather may have left a lot to be desired but it was still only the middle of February and I felt honoured and privileged to be a part of an event which launched the first fairground season of the new millennium.

At around this time I was busy putting the finishing touches to a second civic charity gala show I had been asked to do by the Mayor of North Hykeham, Reg Poole. I felt I must have learned a lot from the previous year's show but in some respects this one was just as difficult when it came to finding suitable acts. The easiest thing to have done would have been to ask everyone who had taken part the previous year, though that wouldn't have been fair to anybody.

But I had an enormous slice of good luck. Sometime earlier I had been introduced to comedian Norman Collier, when he had officially opened North Hykeham Christmas Market. He's an amazing person with a terrific talent and he agreed to top the bill.

With Norman on the show, the rest of the production just fell into place. The venue was switched to the North Kesteven School, which had lots of special memories for me because that was the very first place I had ever presented my juggling act. We may not have sold out but we came pretty close to it, with 270 people in the hall.

As the audience was arriving, organist Norman Ladds entertained at the side of the stage. I once again compered the show and after inviting the Mayor on stage for his opening comments, we followed this with Jazz Vehicle - a talented group of local youngsters who were no mean musicians and it was a great way to start the show.

It took a while to clear the stage so I had to fill in the time with one of the tried and tested jokes from my talk. While singers Dennis Channon and Gill West, accompanied by Jane Foster on the piano, entertained it gave me a chance to change into my El Petanos costume and Lynn and I closed the first half with the Tower of Tumblers, juggling and fire torches.

Having talked to him several times on the phone and done a very good interview which appeared in the Echo, I never had any doubts that Norman would get there exactly on time but it was a big relief, all the same, when he poked his cheerful face around the door and announced his arrival.

When you have got a big name on the top of the bill and you know he has been the reason why most of the people have bought their tickets, it didn't bare thinking about what I would have done if he hadn't turned up on the night. As compere, what on earth could I have said to the audience.

The second half opened with the R.A.F. Waddington Voluntary Pipe Band and our old friend Dee Dee Lee occupying the difficult spot immediately before Norman went on stage.

He was an enormous success and no doubt because of his efforts, the show raised around £1,400 for charity.

A few weeks later at the annual town meeting, Reg was kind enough to present me with the Mayor's Community Shield but I couldn't help thinking that perhaps it ought to have gone to Norman Collier, who had so willingly made the journey from his home on the other side of the Humber Bridge to drive to North Hykeham on a cold February night for the mere pittance we could offer him towards his expenses.

I had been looking forward to my annual appearance at Stamford Mid-Lent Fair for almost the last 12 months and this year it was one of those rare occasions when it fell during the first week in April. When it had taken place in March, the weather had often been pretty grim but this year I thought it would be so much better. The lighter evenings… the spring-like weather… How wrong can you be.

There was snow. There was sleet. There was rain. There was a strong icy wind and it was bitterly cold. Now I love every opportunity to put on my clowning gear and get out there and juggle my fire torches, especially if there is a fair anywhere around. But this time, even I had to admit it was a non-starter and my colleague and I kept our costumes and props in the boot of my car. But I wasn't entirely defeated. On the Saturday afternoon I went back to Stamford again and spent two-and-a-half hours helping to entertain the crowds at the fair, in warm and sunny weather.

Although we hadn't worked on New Year's Eve, millennium celebrations seemed to go on more or less throughout the rest of the year and many an annual event we attended, suddenly had the word "millennium" slotted into its title. From the High Street of Ruskington to the town centre of Clay Cross in Derbyshire and from Newton-on-Trent to Brinsworth we enjoyed our fair share of the millennium celebrations.

One of the more unusual events Lynn and I took part in that summer was at Faldingworth, a village almost mid-way between Lincoln and Market Rasen. A lady, who lived in the village, had come up with the idea of having an annual scarecrow exhibition. In Derbyshire they have their wells dressings. In Spalding they have their tulip festival but in Faldingworth and the adjoining Friesthorpe they have their annual scarecrow exhibition.

And what a wonderful event it was in the year 2000. Villagers were encouraged to make their own scarecrows and dress them up to a different theme every year. Then every morning for a week or so the scarecrows were carried out into the front gardens or the grass verges at the side of the road for the enjoyment of the passing travellers. Then every evening the scarecrows were carried back indoors again until the following day.

A scarecrow trail was produced to guide people around the villages and I have no doubt that it was something of a tourist attraction, probably helping to attract people into the village pubs and shops. That particular year I had been invited to be patron of the exhibition and as something of a little thank you for the honour, I offered to do some entertainment at a teddy bears picnic which was to have been a highlight of the weekend. It should have taken place in the paddock behind one of the pubs but for some reason that I can't remember now, it was brought into the Memorial Hall instead and that probably worked out better for Lynn (as clown Choo Choo) and I because it meant we could actually do a longer show than we could have done outside.

The only snag was, because we had been expecting to do little more than a walk round outside, I hadn't taken my tape recorder and speaker with me, so we had to do the whole show without music.

It was to be one of the last shows Lynn did before she gave birth to our daughter Beth the following September. By coincidence Beth was born in the maternity unit at Lincoln County Hospital at the precise moment the city's September Pleasure Fair was being officially opened on the South Common. It was one of the few times in my adult life, when I have not been at the fair for its official opening - but I think I had a very good excuse on that occasion.

It wasn't long before Beth was being introduced to her "second Daddy", Pedro the Clown. She was only just five weeks old when we took her to see Uncle Sam's American Circus on the South Common and it was for a very good reason - because I was appearing in it. It was a one-off performance dreamed up by ringmaster Gavin Brand. He wanted me, as a local reporter, to take part in the opening night's show, to give it some added publicity. And when I told him I wasn't entirely a stranger to appearing in a circus ring, he couldn't have been more pleased.

Dressed as Pedro, I took part in the clowns' version of the "You can't play here" routine, before being introduced as my real self for a shortened version of my juggling act.

I must admit it felt a bit strange because for once I was taking part in a circus show where I knew no one. Few of the artistes seemed to speak English but at least I got some nods of encouragement before and after my brief appearance.

I began to notice, around this time, a changing pattern in the sort of bookings I was getting. There was still a demand for a circus-type show for parties but I was increasingly being asked to do walk rounds at firework displays, late-night Christmas shoppings and galas.

In the first December of the new millennium I was as busy as ever, but I didn't do a single "show".

One of my new venues and a place which was to become a regular during the next few years, was at a farm just outside the pretty Lincolnshire village of Fillingham. They specialise in selling Christmas trees from a building, which was a barn, successfully converted into a Christmas wonderland.

That first year it may not have been particularly warm. It may not have been particularly well lit but in subsequent years it grew into a terrific place with Santa in his grotto, real life donkeys grazing in their stable, animated figures and traditional hot refreshments. At various times there would be live music and other entertainers strolling around the place, including that amazing man of magic, Paul Derrick, with his bewildering collection of birds.

There would sometimes be a fairground organ playing outside and on one memorable year I was delighted to turn up to find Geoff Woodford's old-time fun fair built up outside for a few weeks.

I had my first opportunity to appear at the new

University of Lincolnshire and Humberside at the end of January 2001 when the Great Australia Day Breakfast moved down from its old home at The Lawn and there must have been close on 1,200 people tucking in to that traditional Australian meal and taking the opportunity to have a look around the new university at the same time. Lynn was with me and using her latest talent - face-painting. When it comes to face-painting, it's one of those things you can either do or you can't and although I may sound biased in this, I have got to say that Lynn is one of the finest face-painters I have ever seen.

But, of course, she lacked confidence at the start, which perhaps wasn't a bad thing. She was half-afraid that some angry parent would take a look at his or her youngster's face and say: "That's terrible! How dare you do such a thing!" But, of course, no one ever did. In fact, it was just the opposite. And while I was walking around juggling with clubs and bean bags and brandishing my tickling stick, Lynn was quietly painting away on the first floor while our baby daughter slept peacefully in the push chair beside her.

I was in Doncaster in mid-February to juggle at the opening of a new supermarket and in the evening I was in New York. That's not the "Big Apple", I am afraid but a small village with the same name in the Lincolnshire Fens. I was juggling with fire torches to an audience of 19 after talking to the Women's Institute in the Village Hall but when you tell people you have appeared in New York it does seem to impress them - as long as you don't go into too many details.

Easter Sunday lunchtime found me at a social club in Wetherby, the little Yorkshire town perhaps best known for its racecourse. I was booked to do 60 minutes and because we couldn't get a baby sitter, I was working on my own. At the time I was worried that I didn't have enough material to fill the whole hour and I had visions of some concert secretary in the corner standing there with a stop-watch in his hand and saying at the end: "You have got to do another five-and-a-half minutes!" But of course there wasn't one and he didn't and by the time I came off stage I was relieved to see I had clocked up the required amount of time.

The following day I was at another little town famous for its races, Market Rasen. This time I was at the racecourse itself helping to entertain a crowd of around 6,000. I was mainly kept busy between the races, keeping the youngsters amused with the juggling. I had never been to the racecourse before, so the whole thing was a bit of a novelty for me and I was thrilled to find I could wonder from enclosure to enclosure and from silver ring to members' area without any official challenging me.

It's amazing what you can get away with when you look ridiculous. I must admit I have never been a great fan of horse-racing but that visit was to be the start of quite a number for me and the only time I felt distressed about anything I saw there was when one of the horses fell badly in front of the grandstand. Officials immediately put up a screen around the fallen horse and I walked away trying to convince myself the horse would make a complete recovery and live to a ripe old age.

That Spring Bank Holiday weekend we should have appeared at Carrington Steam Rally but the event had to be called off. It wasn't the weather this time, but the event was one of quite a few all over the country to fall victim of the Foot and Mouth epidemic, which meant restrictions on people going onto and off farm land.

I had an interesting double in the middle of June - first at a health club promotion for a couple of hours in City Square, right in the heart of Lincoln, at lunchtime and then at the Lincolnshire Aviation Heritage Centre at East Kirkby in the evening.

This was a concert by the Syd Lawrence Orchestra in one of the hangars at the old airfield. Before the concert started, the organisers wanted some strolling entertainers to greet the 900-strong audience as they arrived and I was one of them. The concert took place in front of the centre's Lancaster bomber, called Just Jane. Unlike the Lancaster with the Lincolnshire-based Battle of Britain Memorial Flight, this one doesn't fly but they start up the engines from time to time and taxi along the runway.

I am proud to say I juggled under the wings of the aircraft and immediately in front of its nose - but it goes without saying that I didn't use my fire torches on this occasion. I can just imaging the fuss if I had accidentally set light to it and all those years of aviation history had gone up in flames.

That summer I was booked for a number of galas in the Sheffield and Rotherham area with me doing the clowning and Lynn face-painting. By this time we had lashed out on a small plastic gazebo to protect Lynn from the elements. Sometimes that meant the hot sun but more often than not it meant the wind and the rain.

I couldn't help noticing that, more often than not, Lynn was busy face-painting long after just about the rest of the stallholders had packed up and gone home. It certainly wasn't that she was slow, because she wasn't. I like to think it was because parents and children recognised a good face-painter when they saw one.

Generally the children, even in some of the roughest areas, were well behaved - though I must admit that when we arrived in a strange town, I would always take a close look at the bus shelters and the telephone boxes. If they were badly smashed up or daubed with graffitti, then I feared the worst. But in one community, they were little devils - and that's putting it politely.

There had been some racial trouble the previous evening just a few miles up the road and that didn't make us feel any easier either. The gala was starting with a parade from the local school, down the road and into the park. But when a couple of other entertainers and myself arrived on the street corner, we were alarmed to find we were the only people in the parade.

There was no crowd on the pavement but we were attracting the attention of some very dubious characters. We checked to make sure we were at the right place and when the time came, we set off back to the park. It must have been the smallest carnival parade ever and it didn't help when someone threw a water bomb which went all over one of the entertainers. He went over to them to point out the error of their ways and I held my breath thinking that a fight was going to break out. But the youth backed off and I think spluttered out some kind of apology.

During the carnival, I did a couple of spots first in a big open-sided structure and then in a small tent, while Lynn valiantly face-painted throughout the afternoon.

Apart from not being able to take our eyes off any of our props for a fraction of a moment, the rest of the day passed off peacefully enough but we have never been booked to return to that event and I must admit I am not particularly sorry.

In contrast, the previous day, I had appeared at a lovely little village with the unusual name of Dyke. It's just outside Bourne and there was a parade through the village street finishing up at the Village Hall, where I later did a show. They were really nice people and I was delighted to be invited back a couple of times.

Chapter Twenty One

Laughter After Tragedy

Until that autumn, if anyone had ever asked me the most difficult day I had ever clowned, I would have said without hesitation that it had to be the day of Princess Diana's death in that car crash in Paris. But something in September 2001, ran it pretty close. I was booked to appear at the re-opening of a supermarket in Louth from soon after eight o'clock in the morning the day after the September 11th tragedy in New York.

Everybody had spent the previous day looking at those horrific pictures on television as the World Trade Center crumbled under the terrorist attack and the next morning the daily papers were full of the same thing. And yet, here I was on the streets of Louth trying to make people laugh or at least smile.

Some passersby looked very worried and still in a state of shock, wondering what was likely to happen on the world stage now. There were blank expressions on their faces and they were clearly wrapped up in their own thoughts and worries. But others thought it was a great thing that there was a clown on hand to try to bring a bit of laughter back into their lives and more than one passing motorist sounded his hooter and gave me a cheerful thumbs up.

Because of the tight security which followed September 11th, it meant the postponement of a charity show I was booked to take part in at R.A.F. College Cranwell the next month but it was re-arranged to a later date.

By now we were getting more used to putting up

and taking down Lynn's face-painting gazebo and one of the places she appeared was in the street at the Lincolnshire village of Metheringham for the time-honoured Feast. It's a wonderful event with the village centre closed to traffic for the afternoon and filled with trade and charity stalls and entertainment.

By this time we had devised a way of making the gazebo even more weather-proof by fitting plastic sheets around three sides but we still hadn't solved the problem of how to illuminate the inside once night fell. We briefly explored the possibility of buying a little generator but the cost ruled it out, so once dusk fell at Metheringham, there was no alternative but to put up the closed sign and pack everything away - although there were still a lot of people around.

Later we managed to snatch a few hours after dark by using lights with re-chargeable batteries but even then we were at the mercy of the weather. A few weeks later Lynn was due to face-paint at a firm's fireworks display. Bearing in mind it was early November, this display was to take place on what appeared to be a ploughed field in the middle of nowhere. The wind was whipping across the field, there was a bit of rain and although we got there in plenty of time, we just couldn't get the gazebo up.

We were in danger of seeing the whole thing lifted up into the air and carried off into the gloom by the gale-force wind. In the end, Lynn managed to use one of the stalls provided by the company but it was hardly worth the effort.

The run-up to Christmas once again found us back at Barton-upon-Humber for the two-day festival and I think it was this year that something totally unexpected happened. A highlight of the Saturday was to be a parade with Santa coming through the town centre on a sleigh pulled by a team of dogs. The only snag was, with the minutes ticking away before the start of the parade, the main street through the festival was sealed off by the police.

There had been some sort of incident in one of the buildings and we all wondered what on earth would happen if Santa got there and couldn't get past the blockade. Luckily peace returned to the small North Lincolnshire town just in time for Santa and his followers to go through unheeded.

February of 2002 found Lynn and I back in North Hykeham, as I had agreed to do another gala night for the Mayor's charity. The venue this time was the Robert Pattinson School and once again we had picked a Sunday night in February. Although I had selected almost all the acts myself, I was presented with a ready-made top-of-the-bill in the shape of an attractive all-girl group called Ttorria. They were thoroughly professional but it had crossed my mind that they might be just a little bit too raunchy for an audience made up of people who were mainly past their first flush of youth.

But I needn't have worried. Everybody seemed to enjoy them and in the years to follow I wasn't surprised when the girls went on to international acclaim. Also on the programme with us that year were Judy Theobald, a county poet with the innocence of Pam Ayres and the devilishness of Jo Brand. She was brilliant and we were also very fortunate to have the Bishop Grosseteste College steel band, the Beth Cressell Dancers and the musical Clarke Twins.

Lynn and I did the Tower of Tumblers, juggling and fire, and we were delighted to find out later that the show raised around £1,350 through ticket sales and the raffle.

I was involved in another charity gala in May, by which time security had eased and we were able to stage that postponed show in the Whittle Hall at R.A.F. College, Cranwell. But security wasn't lapse by any means. Apart from doing the Tower of Tumblers and the juggling, I was to compere the show but I hadn't been able to get to the run-through a few days earlier and I arrived to find I didn't have the necessary documents to get me beyond the guardroom.

I waited anxiously in a corner watching the minutes ticking away, as phone call after phone call failed to find anyone who could give me permission to proceed. It all seemed a bit daft, bearing in mind that the first of the audience were beginning to arrive and presumably they didn't need clearance to get into the hall.

Eventually I was allowed to proceed. Thank goodness they hadn't searched my cases and discovered the fire torches and the paraffin. If they had, I would probably still have been in the guard room.

There were 300 people in the audience, including veteran actor Richard Todd, who lived in the county and who will always be known to many of us of a certain age, as Guy Gibson in the 1950s cinema landmark, The Dambusters.

The show gave me another opportunity to work again with Norman Collier and also our old friend Dee Dee Lee. And, just before she went on, Debs confided to me that she was just a little bit nervous because her old dance teacher, Laurence Highton, was in the audience.

He had once taught me to dance at the Castle Ballroom in Lincoln, as well, so at some appropriate time in the show, I made an announcement from the stage and got him to stand up and take a bow. Like so many of his former pupils, I was very sad when he died in a road accident some time afterwards.

There was a lovely post-script to the show when, sometime afterwards, I received a lovely handwritten letter from Richard Todd, who was very complimentary about the production and my part in it. I have no doubt he did it following the request of hard-working Kate Clarricoats, who was behind the whole thing but it was very much appreciated and a souvenir I shall treasure.

Sometimes you get the distinct impression that clowns, like Lynn and I, can be something of a road safety hazard and this was probably true towards the end of April 2002.

One of our young photographers at the Echo was putting together a portfolio and wanted to do this shot with half-a-dozen clowns walking on the top of a hill with him pointing the camera up towards them. He had found the ideal spot at the top of an embankment at the side of a drain in a rural area to the west of Lincoln. The only snag was that the site was visible - perhaps just a little too visible - to drivers on the nearby road running into Lincoln.

We spent a very pleasant hour atop the embankment with most of the passing motorists hooting and waving to us.

I was involved in a very small piece of fairground history in May when Boston Fair was due to open on a Sunday for the first time. To mark the occasion the showmen wanted to create something of a carnival atmosphere, so I was invited to go along and spend a pleasant three hours or so wandering the streets with my juggling props.

Lynn wasn't working with me on that occasion but her fire-eating routine was creating quite a bit of interest and the following weekend, when I was asked to go along and open a summer fair at a church hall in Lincoln, we thought we would do it in a rather novel way. So, with the organisers full approval and accompanied by an Echo photographer, we stood outside the door to the hall and Lynn blew a flame to ignite a paper streamer which was hung across the door.

I had visions of the whole hall going up in smoke but everybody lived to tell the tale.

That was the summer of the Queen's Golden Jubilee celebrations and it was something of a shock to realise that a full quarter-of-a-century had galloped by since the Jubilee celebrations in 1977.

Once again the Jubilee kept me busy for a few days, although Jubilee day itself was a bit of an anti-climax. We were booked for a gala at Bircotes, not far from Bawtry and the weather could hardly have been worse. We managed to get our gazebo up and Lynn was well into her face-painting, when down came the rain and it never let up. Although I spent a couple of hours or so in costume, there was no question of me working, because of the weather and there were no people around anyway. They had all scampered into the nearby social club as soon as the heavens opened.

But funnily enough Lynn was kept hard at it with the face-painting for a full three hours. People were watching her through the windows of the club and as soon as one person moved away, someone else would come running out of the club to be next in the queue.

Most of the events that summer had a "Golden Jubilee" tag attached to their title, including one street party I did in the very attractive Lincolnshire village of Nettleham one Friday evening.

When I took the booking, I must admit I couldn't quite make head nor tail of the information I was given. They wanted a series of shows just five minutes long to groups of around 15 children a time. The idea was that they closed one of the streets to traffic for the evening and had 10 different activities taking place at once. Groups would watch each activity in turn, then every five minutes someone in charge rang a bell or blew a whistle. The group moved on to the next group and the next group took their place. And so it went on from seven o'clock to eight o'clock.

All I could really fit into five minutes was a brief introduction and a quick juggle with a variety of props. Sometimes I was able to use my fire torches and on other occasions I couldn't. The concept seemed to work and thanks to a dry, mild and still evening, a good time seemed to be had by all.

A couple of corporate events followed and they couldn't have been more different from one another.

The first was at North Hykeham where the town's biggest employer, George Fischer, was holding a family fun day on its playing field. We had a terrific time on a field, which at one stage in its history had been home to the old North Hykeham Steam Rally. Lynn toiled away in a tent for more than six hours, transforming the faces of countless children and adults as well. And I walked round the field for hour after hour juggling and generally enjoying the atmosphere of the day and watching something like 2,500 people enjoying themselves on the fairground rides and bouncy castles, which had been provided for their free entertainment.

The next one was totally different. It started with

a bit of a disaster and things never really improved. Very occasionally, mainly because of the large number of things I have to take with me when I go off and do a show, I leave something behind. Sometimes it's important and sometimes it's not so important. I once arrived at a gala without make-up and had to borrow someone's face paints.

I once arrived for a circus show in a small town a dozen miles away from home, only to find I had left my costume hanging up in the wardrobe and I had to make a last-minute dash back for it.

At this particular family day, in the grounds of a very plush hotel on the outskirts of Hull, I arrived to find that while I had quite correctly brought my clown jacket on its hanger, the clown trousers were on another hanger still at home.

It was impossible to drive close on 50 miles home and 50 miles back again for my trousers but luckily one of the other entertainers had a spare pair and she lent them to me. There were around 250 people at the event and to be honest they couldn't have cared less if I had appeared stark naked. When I tried to start my first show in front of one of the tents, nobody took a blind bit of notice and I had to give up in despair after just a few minutes.

At my second attempt, a little later in the afternoon, I amassed an audience that just about made double figures. Luckily I wasn't the only entertainer to suffer from a lack of interest, otherwise I would probably have hung up my oversized clown boots for the last time and called it a day. Why it just never worked, I can't imagine. But I was quite glad when it started to rain and everybody went home early. At least we got paid, so the trip across the costly Humber Bridge and back again hadn't been entirely in vain.

Chapter Twenty Two

Keeping My Feet on the Ground

Occasionally when I am appearing at a fair, someone will ask me to go on one of the rides with them, and if it is at all possible, I will - although I have to be careful of the pitfalls. Aerial rides tend to be a no-no because there's a great danger of losing your wig in mid-air. Even the dodgems can be a little fraught because you are the target for everyone else on the track and if you get too near to the side, someone standing at the edge can easily pull your wig off.

So, ideally I never venture much further than the galloping horses or the cyclone twist, where you can keep one hand on the safety bar and the other on top of your wig.

There was one time when I made an exception to my rule and almost wished I hadn't. John Armitage had bought a new ride called the Polyp. I think it came from one of Butlin's holiday centres and it hadn't travelled for a long time. I hadn't seen one for years let alone had I ever ridden one and when he brought it to Immingham on one of the occasions I was accompanying the civic party around the fair, I looked at it with special interest.

I had mentally ruled out the possibility of riding it in costume because of the problem with the wig, when a couple of youngsters with obvious learning difficulties almost pleaded with me to go on it with them. It would have been impossible to say no, so I spent a literally hair-raising couple of minutes trying to hang on to the wig and the safety bar while the car rose and fell and spun in an alarming way.

I would have no hesitation to go on the ride again but not dressed as a clown.

Only on very rare occasions have I found myself looking at my watch during a performance and wishing that the time would pass more quickly. And one of those occasions was when I found myself booked for a wedding reception at a very smart hotel in east Lincolnshire. I was booked for a three-hour stint - which was far longer than I would have done anyway - combining a show with games and dancing.

I arrived at the venue, carried all my gear through the hotel lobby, along a corridor, round the corner, along another corridor, through a door into a very small lift, out through another door, along another long corridor and into the aerobics studio where I was to work. And because of the amount of props I needed for a full show, I made that journey quite a few times.

Then I discovered my audience of children numbered just 13. Worse still (if that were possible) the ages ranged dramatically. I had children who could hardly have been out of their mother's sight since they were born and I had spotty-faced teenagers who felt they were too old to be with the children and ought to have been downstairs with the grown-ups at the wedding reception.

I managed to spin my 60-minute show out to 70 minutes but the games and dancing were a bit of a nightmare and I was heartily glad when the end of the evening arrived and all the children were ushered downstairs to wave the happy couple off, leaving me with the task of taking everything back to the car again.

If you have never been to Ilkeston Fair, then I have got to tell you, it is well worth a visit. It takes place in the streets of the Derbyshire town in late October, and in 2002 the event was marking its 750th anniversary by opening on a Sunday for the first time. William Wood invited me to go along and clown about in the streets for around three hours, which gave me plenty of time to see the fair.

Unfortunately it turned out to be one of the coldest and wettest Sundays of the year. It started raining during the open-air service in the Market Place and it carried on throughout the rest of the afternoon. There weren't a lot of people about but my biggest fear was that Nottingham Forest and Derby County were playing against each other that day and the people of Ilkeston seemed to be divided in their loyalties. As far as I could make out, half the town supported one team and the other half supported the other.

I had feared there might be some trouble at the fair after the game but there were plenty of police around, so I escaped with nothing more than a drenching.

It was at this fair I met a couple of lovely fairground fans. They took a few pictures of me and said they would send me some copies in due course. Lots of people say this but very few actually do bother to do it but this couple did and the pictures provided me with a nice souvenir of the day.

When it came to getting wet, the run-up to that Christmas took a lot of beating. The final day of Barton-upon-Humber Christmas Festival had coincided with a downpour and I remember juggling to an almost deserted street, as I sheltered under the awning of a fairground fun house. At North Scarle, a normally quiet little rural village close to the Lincolnshire/Nottinghamshire border, it rained more or less throughout the whole of the village feast.

I remember sitting in my car, parked at the end of the main street, watching the rain beating against my windscreen as I waited for the time to come for me to go back and make my next appearance, and thinking to myself "What on earth am I doing working outside this time of year? Why aren't I appearing in some nice cosy, dry club or theatre?"

The summer of 2003 is perhaps best remembered for the different kinds of places I appeared. Lynn and I were at a new Tesco store in Horncastle on Spring Bank Holiday Saturday when, I must confess, I kept slipping back to my car during the afternoon to hear how Lincoln City were getting on in the Fourth Division play-off at Cardiff. Somehow I managed to keep smiling despite City's eventual defeat.

The next couple of days I was on the back of an open-sided lorry at Carrington Steam Rally. Then I was at a Lincoln community centre, a rural churchyard as part of a village arts and music festival in the grounds of a country house and on a school playing field.

While appearing at Birchwood Leisure Centre in Lincoln, I met the guest of honour, Nick Knowells. Now, with all due respect to him, I have to admit I had never heard of Nick Knowells. It turned out he was best known as a television handyman, which probably accounted for why I had never heard of him because, being nothing of a handyman myself, I tend to avoid "house makeover" and DIY programmes like the plague.

But he was a real nice chap and, when he finished what he had to do, he came round the back of the hall to watch one of my shows. Afterwards, he told me he could juggle so I immediately handed him my clubs and, when I discovered he was no mean juggler, I persuaded him to take part in the next show of the afternoon and he was a big hit.

It was around this time I had brought a new prop into my act. Mobile phones had by this time gone from being the pride and joy of the yuppies to the point when just about every man, woman and child had at least one - even if he couldn't manage to use it properly. I worked out that, if I could manage to juggle with three mobile phones, it would be something that everyone - no matter what age - could identify with.

Just finding the mobile phones was no easy task. We had an old one at home but I was unable to discover any charity shops which sold them. Eventually a friend at work, whose family must have got through a fair number of mobile phones in a very short space of time, came up with more than I could possibly use at once.

After a lot of practicing, and smashing more than one on the ground, I succeeded in doing what I had intended and the mobile phones have been a part of my show ever since.

Later that summer I did three question and answer sessions and mini-shows at a village school not far from Lincoln. It was a lovely relaxed session when I had a number of interesting questions from the under 10-year-olds, including one from a youngster who wanted to know if I was married. And a few weeks later a large bundle of letters and pictures arrived from the children, saying how much they had enjoyed my lesson. It took a long time but I managed to reply to them all.

The same week I spent the Saturday back at Dyke

Summer Fair before going on to Tolethorpe Hall open-air theatre just outside Stamford. It's the home of the Stamford Shakespeare Company and, when they had asked me to join the company for one night, it was an offer I couldn't refuse. But I wasn't going to appear on the stage in one of Shakespeare's finest. It was their annual summer event and, before the curtain went up, the audience spent a couple of hours or more having a glass of two of champagne at a picnic on the lawn. The weather really excelled. It was hot. It was sunny. The sky was blue and everyone was in the party spirit.

There were other strolling players mixing and mingling with the crowds as well and I remember a group of Morris Men press-ganged me into joining them for one of their dance routines. Now, if I am honest, I have never been mad keen on Morris Men but they went up in my estimation after that routine, because it's not as easy as it might look and you must have to keep yourself pretty fit for it.

There aren't many clowns who can boast their warm-up act has been the rock legends Status Quo but I am afraid I have been known to say that - although I might be slightly guilty of bending the truth. Quo were appearing on an outdoor stage in the grounds of Lincoln Castle on August Bank Holiday Monday. Lynn and I had the day off so we were among the audience and it was a great night.

The next lunchtime I was appearing at the castle during one of their regular family fun days. Quo had finished their spot sometime after ten o'clock that night and I was the next act to go on, at lunchtime the following day. Though it has got to be said the reception I received was far quieter than Quo's.

After a summer of carnivals and family days, the

autumn took me to Ripley Charter Fair for the first time. The Market Place, where most of the fair takes place, is alleged to be the highest Market Place in the whole of Derbyshire. I wouldn't doubt it for one moment and by the middle of October it was a trifle chilly. So the showmen have this wonderful tradition of serving up what they call "a hot toddy" on the dodgem track at the civic opening.

As always, when I am booked for a town centre fair, parking was a problem and I couldn't get changed and made-up in a caravan, because they all seemed to be parked too far away from the fair. So there was nothing for it but to change and make up in my car parked alongside the pavement in a residential area. It was getting dusk, so even if there had been anyone walking by, I don't think they would have seen anything they shouldn't have seen. But any householder, gazing out of his front room window, might have raised an eyebrow or two if he saw me entering the car as a normal person, and coming out again a few minutes later, dressed as a clown.

I think it was either that year or the next, when there was something of a technical hitch with the civic opening. The Mayor didn't seem to arrive at the time he was expected, so I was handed the microphone and told to keep the crowd entertained for a few minutes. It seemed to be a very long time for me and I suspect the people in the crowd as well, until the Mayor arrived to do the honours.

The following year the ceremony almost didn't go ahead at all because a man was involved in some sort of rooftop protest on a building overlooking the fair and, if he had still been in that position at the time of the opening ceremony, it wouldn't have been allowed to continue. But I think one of the showmen went up onto the roof and explained to the man in no uncertain terms that he ought to go back down again. The protestor took his advice and the fair went ahead as planned.

In 2004, after two years at the University of Lincolnshire and Humberside, the Great Australian Breakfast returned to its old home at The Lawn and the opening hours had been trimmed back to a more respectable time. Now, we were starting shortly before nine o'clock and closing at 12.30p.m. and we were still managing to get something like 1,000 people in.

This was the 13th event of its kind and it gave me an opportunity to give Pedro a slightly different look. I had bought myself a new wig and I had finally pensioned off my old oversize boots. They had started to wear very badly and I didn't expect to get through another year with them. So I had re-discovered an old pair of brown boots which I had cast off some years ago. I gave them a couple of coats of paint - one predominantly blue and the other predominantly red - and found to my delight that not only did they look pretty good but I could drive in them as well.

A sunny Sunday in May found me at the Portland Training College for the disabled on the edge of Mansfield. I had never been there before but I knew a bit about it because through my work at the Echo, I used to have dealings with a retired police inspector, who had done a lot to raise money for the college.

They were staging a horticulture and craft day and I was booked to do two 35-minute shows inside the Leisure Centre. The people couldn't have been nicer and it turned out to be one of the most pleasant afternoons of the summer.

Over the Spring Bank Holiday weekend, I was

again booked for Carrington Steam Rally, working on the mobile stage with the very talented Schuhplattlergruppe from Boston Grammar School. Under the direction of one of their teachers, Richard Anderson, the team of boys dress in traditional German-style costumes. There's lots of knee slapping, dancing, acrobatics, humour and even some wood chopping.

I watched them two or three times each day, between my own spots and was very impressed with their enthusiasm and skills. But they did present me with a bit of a problem, because I had to announce them at the start of every performance and somehow I just couldn't get my tongue round their name.

The result was I made a dreadful job of doing it, and I think that on one occasion I even introduced them as members of the Boston Philatelic Society. But they didn't seem to mind.

Towards the end of a summer of galas and carnivals the weather didn't seem to be getting cooler. If anything it was getting hotter and, when I appeared at the Boston Town and Miniature Steam Show in Central Park, during the first weekend in September, it was really scorching. I was working on a big stage facing directly into the sun, and by the time I had finished my second spot, I felt as if I had just run a marathon or taken part in an FA Cup Final.

Apart from my own spots, I also had the job of commentating on a parade of llamas in the main ring. Now, apart from the fact that you found them in a lot of circuses and occasionally spotted them looking out at you over a farmers hedge somewhere, I didn't know a lot about llamas - well, you don't, do you. So someone thoughtfully provided me with some written information about them and people in the crowd must have been very impressed by the expert knowledge of this clown, who seemed to know everything there was to know about llamas. I hope they didn't notice the notes half-hidden in my hand.

A couple of weeks later I juggled on Lincoln South Common on the opening night of the city's September Pleasure Fair. The event had started as a holiday-at-home fair during the Second World War, so at the time it was just a little over 60 years old and it was nice to think that in all those years I was probably the first clown to juggle at the event.

The autumn found me on the wide-open spaces of the County Showground near Lincoln, where the city's four Rotary clubs had got together to organise a Family Fireworks and Fun Spectacular. Singer and actress, Barbara Dickson, was among the special guests and thanks to one of the mildest November evenings you could imagine, a crowd of around 11,000 turned up.

It was a wonderful event and hopefully laid the foundations for a lot more to come.

My eagerly-awaited visit to Lapland on the BBC Radio Lincolnshire flight dominated my pre-Christmas that year and after that there was time only for a visit to Scunthorpe and to a Christmas Market in Wisbech, before the festive season arrived.

It was showman Donald Gray, who had been responsible for getting me my last booking of the old year and by coincidence the first booking of the New Year. I was back at King's Lynn Mart again, this time as a very small part of the town's 800th charter celebrations.

This time I drove all the way there and all the way back again in costume, which is something I don't really like doing in case the car breaks down on the journey. Worse still, when I arrived in the town on a very cold and miserable day, there was nowhere to park. I kept driving further and further away from the fair and in the end I found a space in a multi-storey car park about 10 minutes walk away.

And what a long 10 minutes that seemed to be. When people see a clown at a carnival or fair, they are not at all surprised. But if you happen to see one getting out of a car in a multi-storey car park and setting off to walk through the town, it's a totally different story. I mean, when did you last see a clown walk out of a multi-storey car park?

Because of the weather, the fair was a lot quieter than it ought to have been and at the end of the afternoon I had that long walk back to the car park again.

Parking could have been something of a problem at my next venue as well but I had a stroke of luck. In the centre of Lincoln there used to be a corporation bus garage, which, in the fullness of time, was demolished to make way for a big block of flats for students from the university. As far as I could see, parking outside the flats was at a premium but I was fortunate because the building adjoined the Echo office and I could park quite easily in the space where I left my car from Monday to Friday.

The event was a five-year-old's birthday party and, because it was still a fairly new building, I was almost certainly the first entertainer to appear in the common room there.

Sometime earlier I had been asked to do another charity show for the Mayor of North Hykeham and this time, because it was becoming increasingly difficult to ask artistes to give up a Sunday evening for nothing, I thought I would try something a little different. I contacted my new friends from Boston Grammar School and they readily agreed to take part in the show. (You see, I have carefully managed to avoid using their name again because I can never successfully spell it without making two or three attempts first).

With the boys earmarked as the finale act, I decided to call the show, "A Celebration of Youth" and set about filling the stage with a total of 100 young people.

Yes, it sounds fairly easy doesn't it but it turned out to be more difficult than I had expected. With the Starlite Twirlers, the Ready Steady Choir, Devaney School of Irish Dance and young musicians Joseph Sayed, Arif Sayeed and Graham Blyth and the Lincolnshire Army Cadet Force Band, I was nearing my 100-target. But I was still short of comedy. In the end the problem was solved by a group of students from a drama course at Lincoln College, who performed a number of sketches and went down well.

The venue this time was the Terry O'Toole Theatre at North Hykeham and we managed to raise close on £900 for good causes. The theatre had a smaller seating capacity than either of the town's main school halls and I expected there would be no difficulty at all in selling all the tickets. But again, it wasn't as easy as it sounds.

I had confidently expected that for every child taking part there would be two parents and possibly aunts, uncles, brothers and sisters, who would buy tickets to see them. Unfortunately they didn't. Worse still, some mums and dads watched from the side of the auditorium, when their own youngsters were on the stage and when their spot was finished, they took their children straight home without stopping to see the rest of the show. So there was a constant coming and going throughout the show, which must have been a bit distracting for those people who had paid for their tickets to see the whole thing.

A garden centre on the outskirts of the small market town of Horncastle provided an unusual venue for me during the early part of the summer and again in the run-up to Christmas. They were long days, starting at ten o'clock in the morning and going through until four o'clock but they were generally happy days and I could roam freely around the garden centre creeping up on unsuspecting members of the public, who never expected to see a clown among the shrubs and plants.

The morning was generally spent outside the main entrance, if the weather was good, welcoming visitors as they got out of their cars. Later in the day, I would walk around the garden centre and towards the end of the afternoon I would be somewhere near the check-out thanking the customers for coming and saying we hoped they would come and see us again. At least one of the customers seemed to be under the impression that I was the owner, who liked to dress up as a clown and mingle with the customers to find out what they really thought about the place.

As the Spring Bank Holiday weekend arrived, I was becoming increasingly conscious that my 60th birthday was fast approaching. I might have found it just a little bit more difficult than usual to get on and off the high stage at the Carrington Steam Rally but I tried not to show it. Once again, the event was plagued by heavy showers and a thunderstorm and heavy rain was falling as I did my second show of the day.

I watched for a few minutes as a handful of people

sat huddled under their umbrellas and stepped forward to the edge of the stage. Did they want me to stop so they could go off somewhere and find cover? Not a bit of it. They had sat out there so long in the rain they didn't think they could get any wetter and they wanted the show to carry on. By that time, the rain had made the edge of the stage very wet and slippery, so 1 was particularly careful that I didn't disappear over the edge and land fairly and squarely in the laps of the people sitting on the front row.

At the end of the show, the boys from Boston Grammar School had a surprise for me. They called me back on stage and presented me with a 60th birthday card, which they had all signed and a bottle of wine as well. Of all the presents and cards I received, they were among the most special.

There was no rain a few weeks later when I appeared at Boston Party in the Park. In fact, a little rain would have been welcoming because the temperatures were soaring and I was certainly feeling the heat. I make a point of never taking my jacket off during a walk-round. It's very much a part of the costume, and I always think that Pedro isn't Pedro without it. But I was very tempted to leave it back in my car that day.

It's very much an annual event and it had got to be among the most successful in the town's calendar. It takes place in Central Park. There's a free gate and a procession of bands working on a stage throughout the day. There's a pretty big fair and on this particular day it looked as though the whole town had turned out.

It started quietly though and I found myself briefly the target of some young troublemakers, who thought it would be fun to grab my wig and run off with it. When that sort of thing happens - and it does from time to time - I am in a very difficult position. Pedro needs his wig and yet he can't be seen to chase off after the offenders and try to wrestle it from their grasp. On this particular occasion however, it was one of the fairground employees, who came to my aid and retrieved the wig along with a stern warning to the offenders not to try it again.

In September I was invited to officially open Lincoln Pleasure Fair as Pedro. I had done it a few years earlier, at the request of Councillor David Jackson, who had been booked to do the honours but when he spotted me among the crowd he thought it would be nice, if I joined him for the ceremony.

This time I was to open the fair myself from the platform of one of the rides. After making a brief speech and presenting a couple of competition winners with their prizes, I rang the twin bells to officially declare the fair open. Then, following in the footsteps of all the mayors and important people who had done it before, I went off on a tour of the fair, trying out several of the rides, including some I had never been on before.

Just in case it might have escaped your notice, 2005 was the 400th anniversary of the Gunpowder Plot. Yes, I didn't know that either until one of the organisers of the second annual fireworks spectacular on the County Showground, told me. One of my tasks at the event was to judge a Guy Fawkes competition but unfortunately the task was made even more difficult by the fact that there weren't any entries. Robbed of my moment of glory!

It was during the run-up to Christmas that I experienced one of those particularly memorable moments. I was booked to appear at a children's party in a social club. I think in the good old days it would have been referred to as a "working men's club" but in the new millennium the name had been changed to "social club" - possibly because few of the members were working and most were on the social.

When I arrived, I pushed my way into the hall and I almost had to part the cigarette smoke with my hands to get in. One of the committee took one look at me and announced in no uncertain terms: "The turn's arrived!"

I hadn't been called "a turn" for years. The stage was one of those pocket handkerchief ones and once I had finished my spot I had to get off pretty smartish to make room for Santa Claus. And all the while, despite the fact the hall was almost completely full of children, the place seemed to be enveloped in a permanent cloud of cigarette smoke. I tried not to breathe too deeply while I was there and did my best to put the phrase "passive smoking" out of my mind.

As 2006 dawned I little expected that within weeks I would be bidding a fond farewell to the Echo. But these things happen, and sometimes sooner than we expect.

I haven't got to the stage yet of strolling past the Echo building, gazing up longingly at the windows and saying to myself: "I wish I was back there," because I don't.

It really was time to move on but I don't regard myself as retired or even semi-retired. Self-employed is how I like to describe myself, although I am to some extent a house husband and the school run keeps me occupied weekday mornings and afternoons.

Apart from that, at the City Council's request, I have re-created the old Gossiper page on the council's website. I research the bygone newspapers for Dave

Bussey's "Hits and Headlines" feature on BBC Radio Lincolnshire and I am heard briefly on air five afternoons a week. I am still writing for the World's Fair and doing a limited number of "after dinners" and talking at meetings.

And I am still keeping myself busy as Pedro as well. As I wrote in the footnote to my very last Gossiper page in the Echo on February 18, 2006: "If, at some future date, you happen to spot a strange-looking character with make-up, red curly wig, clad in an outrageous suit, and juggling a set of fire torches, don't forget to say hello - because it just might be me."